Dedicated to my wonderful family

Kerri, Nathan and Brendan

© 2015 Malcolm Guy

# Boost Your Team's Productivity by Reducing Workplace Conflict

Stop disputes escalating while creating your winning team culture

By Malcolm Guy

# Index

| Introduction | Page |
|---|---|

| | | |
|---|---|---|
| 1 | How I Got to Where I Am | 1 |
| 2 | A Great Place to Start Boosting Your Productivity | 10 |
| 3 | Changing Corporate Culture from the Bottom Up | 18 |
| 4 | The Cost of Re-Employment | 23 |
| 5 | How Workplace Relationships Affect Productivity | 29 |
| 6 | Mind Mapping and Brainstorming Conflict | 34 |
| 7 | Dealing with Difficult People | 46 |
| 8 | Bullying and How to Maintain a Reliable Workplace Policy | 54 |
| 9 | Dealing with Recurring Conflict Issues | 66 |
| 10 | The Conflict Continuum - Hidden Costs of Avoidance and Wasted Time in Conflict | 77 |
| 11 | The Monetary Cost of Conflict | 93 |
| 12 | What's Your Dispute Resolution Plan and Where Does Mediation Fit? | 107 |
| 13 | Stopping the Head hunters - or At Least Slowing Them Down | 125 |
| 14 | Gardening – Conclusion | 138 |

I really appreciate receiving feedback on this book, and I would love your input to make the next version even better. Please leave me a helpful review on Amazon or email me at [malguy@mimmediation.net](mailto:malguy@mimmediation.net) letting me know what you thought of the book.

Thanks so much,

                    Malcolm

# Acknowledgements

There have been many people who have helped me along my journey to get this book published. From family and friends, to business partners and teachers, everyone I have spoken to and dealt with has had an impact in what has ended up in this book.

Specifically I want to thank my wife, Kerri, our boys Nathan and Brendan and my extended family all over the world now. Others I want to specifically mention are Ken Young, Joanne Law, Colin Andrew, Jadie Hunter, Aled Davies & Tina Thomas.

To all the others that I haven't mentioned here, you are all important to me and have helped shape the man that I am today.

# Disclaimer

Although the author has made every effort to ensure that the information in this book was correct at press time, the author does not assume and hereby disclaim any liability to any party for any loss, damage, or disruption caused by errors or omissions, whether such errors or omissions result from negligence, accident, or any other cause.

# Introduction

In today's busy workplace, conflict can steal much of your day. Do you get interrupted constantly with other people's issues and disputes, wasting your time dealing with unproductive conflict? Is staff turnover like a revolving door? Would you rather spend your working days developing and nurturing a culture that you and your staff enjoy being a part of?

This book gives you the strategies to develop a team culture that other managers will envy. This book will also show you proven ways to enhance team communication, and share effective techniques to develop more beneficial and productive working environments. This book is for managers and leaders who want to inspire, make their business more profitable, and do this in a more gratifying environment. After all, who wants to spend time working in cold, hostile or unpleasant surroundings?

As a lifetime learner and an expert in resolving conflict, I have been refining my personal communication philosophy my entire life. I have managed both small and large teams with great effectiveness to focus their efforts, along with whole companies to maintain their positive culture for prolonged periods. Within my family we have had to deal with the unsolved murder of my nephew, which lead me to volunteer as a telephone crisis counsellor at Lifeline Melbourne. At Lifeline I speak 'one on one' to people during their personal crisis at their most vulnerable times. Because of, and as an extension of my Lifeline experience, I have become an accredited mediator. I've grown my business to help support people just like you to become better communicators and leaders, guiding them to the creation of higher productivity.

By learning and implementing the strategies and techniques in this book, I believe that team leaders, entrepreneurs and managers will see improvements across their workplace in productivity and staff retention. These easy to implement strategies and techniques create a friendlier working environment, while engaging in more effective and productive conversations. I know that the methods and strategies listed in the following pages reduce workplace stress and increase staff enthusiasm, which flows though into a better work/life balance in general. Who doesn't want that?

As Jadie, a well-respected program manager from Melbourne said, "I find Malcolm's recommendations very useful in dealing with conflict resolution in the volunteer sector. The best thing about his advice is that it includes simple, practical strategies that I can implement into my workplace straight away."

I promise if you follow even just a few of the tips and suggestions in this book, you will enjoy the benefits of reduced conflict at work, and be able to spend more time working on projects and tasks that actually matter to you and your company. As an added benefit, once your staff and team are seen to be working more cohesively, your peers and managers will start questioning what you have accomplished, and how you have achieved those amazing results. Then you will become an even more valuable employee.

Einstein said, "The definition of insanity is doing the same thing over and over and expecting different results". Conflict is no different.

The strategies and techniques in this book can be implemented quickly and easily, and the changes in patterns that will happen to you and those around you, will amaze and inspire you. Be the leader you know you want to be, someone who others look to and aspire to be like. Be that person who takes action.

The conflict management principles and strategies you are about to learn are proven to create long-term positive results. If you want to reduce your stress levels, you need to learn something new to create a better workplace environment and continue improving.

Each chapter will give you new insights as you become more aware of the simple changes you can make in your day-to-day working life. Take control right now, make every day more productive than the last while enjoying the new life and team you will create.

# Chapter 1

# How I Got to Where I Am

I grew up on a dairy farm in New Zealand, in a large family, but as the youngest of six children I was left to myself a lot of the time. There was plenty of time spent working on the farm, and it was a great place to grow up. As I grew though, I knew it wasn't where I was destined to stay. There seemed to be so much more to explore and I left home at 18, ready to take on the world.

## My first negotiation

I do remember convincing two very shy farm workers from Samoa to play guitar and sing for us one night. The family knew they had great voices as we'd heard them singing together privately, but they were very shy and hardly knew anyone else at my brother's 21$^{st}$ party that night. Put simply, I got the men to agree to perform because I convinced both of them separately that the other had already agreed.

They were surprised when they came together and realised what I'd done, but they sang a few beautiful songs in perfect harmony before slinking away again. Plenty of others in the family had already asked them to sing that night, but I was the one to make it happen. I like to think of that as my earliest successful negotiation involving adults; I was 14.

## Leaving Home

By the time I was 25 I'd moved to Australia, where I settled into 10 years of managing operations and logistics for a start-up spring water company. I was their first employee in Melbourne, and we had prolonged and dynamic growth of around 30% per annum for many years once we became established. That's where I developed my personal management style of open communication. It just seemed the natural and respectful way to deal with people to me. Maybe it was my upbringing on the farm, my boss at the time, or maybe it's just in my genes.

## Moving On

I left the spring water company in 2001 and run construction businesses on my own and in partnerships, along with a number of other side ventures. I'd had plenty of ups and downs along the way. I met and married the love of my life and together we grew our family to include two wonderful boys.

In 2010 I received a phone call from my brother that rocked our world to the core. My nephew had been shot, and he died in his driveway on his way to the morning milking. I missed the initial call from my brother in New Zealand that morning, and I forget the actual message he left, but I knew something was dreadfully wrong. When I called back my niece answered the phone, and she was sobbing terribly as she told me how her brother had been ambushed early that morning on his way to milking, shot in his driveway and left for dead.

The family rallied around and my wife and I flew out the next day to be with my brother and the rest of my NZ family. Our boys were 11 & 9 at the time, and we told them what we knew, believing that telling them the truth (as we knew it) was the best for everyone.

The story was headline news in NZ. Who had shot Scott; a 30 year farmer, with a beautiful wife, an 18 month old boy and another baby on the way? There wasn't a lot we could do but be there for each other. My sister-in-law changed overnight, declaring how she felt that her heart had been ripped out. My brother took the lead and fronted many news conferences over the next few weeks and months.

The police interviewed the immediate family for hours, some of them several times. They called on the public for help and information. There were many theories and suspects, but no arrest for 8 months.

## The Second Shock

When an arrest was made it sent another shock wave through the family, and again made the headlines. The police had arrested Scott's brother-in-law, his sister's husband, with whom he had worked closely on the family dairy farm.

Scott's parents, Bryan and Joanne, were faced with too many questions without answers. They were attempting to understand what was happening to them and their family. Fortunately, they have been able to draw on strength from within, and continue to be great role models for the extended family. They also speak publicly and give support in the community to others who have been through similar tragedies of violent crime. The last five years have been an incredible journey for them and their offspring, and they continue to remain positive about the future and set wonderful examples for everyone around them. Joanne and Bryan's experience is told in a gripping read that also imparts tools on dealing with the vagaries of life, and can be found at: http://www.amazon.com.au/Scott-Guy-Parents-Betrayal-Courage-ebook/dp/B00GRXV1ZC/ref=cm_cr_pr_pb_opt?ie=UTF8

Joanne and her daughter Anna also have a website and blog regularly on their insights, struggles, mountains climbed and

what to do when life sends you a whole lot of lemons.
http://makelemonade.co.nz/

## Back in Melbourne

During the ensuing months between the murder and the arrest, I was back in Melbourne with my family continuing our daily routines, unable to help or be near my family. I'd regularly find myself drifting through all the possible combinations of why, who, what happened that day, while isolated in another country and unable to do anything to help.

It was during this time, while I was working for the Australian Red Cross, that an urgent request for volunteers to help on the phones came through the office. Red Cross offers a service to connect people who have been separated during natural disasters or war, and I was asked to take part in the team of volunteers. It was the 2010 Queensland Christmas floods, and I was quite willing to help out. So with very little training, I was on the phones speaking to strangers at their time of crisis; people who didn't know where their loved ones were. I was let into the lives of people at a time when they were very frightened and uncertain about what was happening to them, and their loved ones. It was the first time I was given permission by a stranger to hear their deepest fears, and listen to what they were scared of.

While a few of the calls were confronting and distressing, I realised that I had helped callers just by listening to their story. Here I was, a stranger at the end of a phone line that they would never meet or talk to again, and yet they opened up to me, their life and deepest fears. It was a strangely comforting experience, knowing that I was able to reduce someone's anxiety during an uncertain time, from a phone room hundreds of km's away. Over the next few weeks I found myself thinking more and more about those conversations, and what it meant to the callers to have somebody to talk to when they were in crisis and needed someone to listen.

## My First Call to Lifeline

A few weeks later I phoned Lifeline Melbourne and enquired about volunteering on their crisis phone line. Lifeline runs their crisis line for anyone to call and talk about whatever crisis is happening to them, right at that time. All calls to Lifeline are anonymous, confidential and free. It is a fantastic service that has been operating 24/7 since 1964. Most of the people on the phone are volunteers giving up their time to help others in their time of need. In writing this book, I am careful not to breach any confidentiality discussing individual calls, but I do discuss the issues I come across with others.

By talking to my family and others about people's challenges, I hope to inform them that there is help for people who ask for it at any time. I also believe it's good for my kids to know that lots of people have difficulty in dealing with different aspects of their life, and that there is always someone to talk to.

I believe that my work with Lifeline does help people, and that at times it is enough to stop callers carrying out actions that they would regret. Most often that involves simply talking to people and sometimes just keeping them safe for now.

## Exploring Options

Part of the work that we do at Lifeline is exploring options with callers. We are not there to tell them what to do, because the best way for people to work through their crisis is to come up with the solutions themselves. We might offer suggestions to question and challenge some of their behaviour, but in the end, the caller needs to realise their options and decide what is best for them. Whether it's at Lifeline or life in general, when people believe that they have found the solution themselves, they are more likely to follow through with action.

I had been at lifeline for about two years when I decided that the next natural progression in my career was to become a qualified mediator and expand the crisis phone-line skills into a career. Since becoming a nationally accredited mediator I have been effectively working to reduce conflict in the workplace, and training others to do this too. It became apparent pretty quickly that by reducing people's conflict, their productivity increased significantly as a result. This in turn has got me where I am today, and to writing this book for you.

## Lifeline Awareness Talks

Along with my conflict resolution business, I also deliver Lifeline awareness presentations to companies and youth groups. I really enjoy delivering these presentations as there are still a lot of people unaware that Lifeline even exists, especially among the youth groups I speak to. I've spoken to Scout Venturer and Rover groups where participants are aged between 15 and 25, and at a vulnerable age. It surprises me how very few of these young people are aware that Lifeline exists, so to be able to explain to them that there is help at the end of a phone or on a chat-line is very worthwhile.

I had a mother approach me a few days after one of these youth presentations. She told me that her 16 year old son came home the night of my presentation and talked to her about Lifeline. I'm very proud when any 16 year old boy goes home after one of my presentations and talks to his mother, even better when the discussion is about suicide awareness and mental health. It is a very rewarding part of my work when families engage like that.

The strategies and opinions offered in these pages are those that I have been using to help people create an improved and more productive life at work, and in their personal situations. Work-life balance can be a constant struggle. However, with the right tools and attitude you can improve your current situation. This book is not only about increasing productivity, it's about enriching your life so that you can become a more fulfilled person.

We are all where we are today because of the choices we have made in the past. To create a better future for tomorrow, we need to make wiser, more informed choices today.

## Chapter 2

# A Great Place to Start Boosting Your Productivity

Have you struggled with having difficult conversations in the workplace and then realised that not dealing with these situations doesn't make them disappear? If so, you're in the right place.

Here are the 8 most significant topics we will discuss in the following chapters. This book will help you to change the way you interact with colleagues and improve your working life.

### Getting used to difficult conversations

Having difficult conversations makes some people very nervous and uncomfortable. Not having them, however, doesn't make them go away. The earlier you have the conversation, the sooner you can solve the underlying issues.

## Creating open minded workplaces

Imagine a workplace that's full of conflict, where people spend too much time and energy building up defences against others because they can't get past what someone said or how they were treated. That doesn't sound like an ideal place to work and probably not where you would choose to work either.

What do you think happens to the person who brings new ideas or concepts into a workplace full of conflict? I believe they either get shut down, not given the time to be heard, or leave the company of their own accord because of the environment. The biggest improvement for your company might never even be discussed because of your workplace culture.

Now consider a workplace where staff feel comfortable talking to each other and their manager about any topic. Visualise your workplace as a breeding ground of great ideas – a place where staff are comfortable enough to raise concerns and issues about their colleagues. This is a place where others want to work, and where those who already work there enjoy prospering and spending time with like-minded people.

That's what I'm talking about when I say, 'Reducing workplace conflict will increase your productivity'.

## Wasting time in conflict

I'm not saying that you are going to eliminate all conflict around your workplace. In fact, a certain level of conflict will always be present and is actually needed to produce new ideas and stimulate growth. Without people challenging the norm or the current way of thinking, we would still be back in the dark ages in many respects.

Not dealing with disputes as they arise only compounds the issues – it doesn't make them go away. People will naturally talk about their concerns to colleagues. When those concerns aren't heard by the right people (i.e. managers who can produce solutions), concerns escalate into disputes and continue escalating.

## The conflict continuum

This is where the wasted time starts to build up. Staff start talking about the issue around the coffee machine. People not previously involved get drawn into discussions and take sides. When left unresolved, what began as a small dispute builds and grows into something with a life of its own, consuming large amounts of time and energy that should be spent on actual productive ideas and activities. Senior managers and HR get drawn in and they all need to be briefed as well. Administration procedures need to be followed and completed. Mediators may be engaged from time to time and if mediation doesn't reach a successful conclusion, litigation may be the next step.

All those steps consume many, many hours of valuable time, during which nothing constructive is actually happening. All that time has been wasted talking and working to resolve a conflict that should have been dealt with in the early stages.

There are ways of creating an environment where people feel respected and comfortable to talk openly about anything.

## Brainstorming and mind mapping

Brainstorming and mind mapping are ideas that are often thought of as simple and out-dated. I believe they are in fact useful management tools that are under-utilised. While they are very simple, they are extremely effective tools when used correctly – whether it's in a group situation where you want to get everyone's input displayed quickly on a white board, or when you want to get ideas out of your head and onto paper where you can visualise them simply, and show them to others.

## Stand up-coffee meetings

This is another simple idea, but just because these ideas are simple, please don't exclude them from your toolbox. The objective is to get everyone talking in an informal situation, so that when people have more important or difficult topics to discuss, they feel comfortable. When people feel comfortable talking about the smaller issues, they are more likely to discuss the significant ones.
The idea is to have a brief 15 or 20 minute coffee meeting and be able to talk to anyone in the team. It should be a stand-up meeting so that people are free to move in and out of conversations as they choose. It's also a way of including shy or more introverted people in group discussions. These introverts often have plenty of ideas, but feel uncomfortable expressing them. Simply getting them involved in stand-up coffee meetings can make them feel more at ease talking to other team members.

## Why staff leave their jobs

This chapter is important as it will help you clarify why staff leave and what you can do about it. One of the main reasons people leave their job is because of their direct manager – the person who has the most impact on their work. Their direct manager sets their work load, their deadlines and expectations, and that is who they are accountable to. Unless there is a healthy and strong working relationship between staff and the direct manager, sooner or later people start looking for a new job.

I know nowadays people change jobs much more often than in the past, and that offers new possibilities in how we can interact with staff. Consider developing a working relationship where you can discuss more than simply the current projects, and work towards an employment model that sets up the ability to grow healthy, strong, open relationships with staff.

While you may never know a staff member's entire agenda, you might be surprised how open some people are to discussing long term goals and aspirations. You can actually ask people indirectly how long they intend to stay with the company, through open questions about their intentions once you have their trust.

People may be naturally suspicious if their manager were to ask if they are thinking of leaving the company and I can see why. However, if that manager knew the employee well enough and they were comfortable talking about this, why not?

Then, throughout the employee's work span with you, you could have regular conversations about how long they intend to stay, what training might make them stay longer and what else is going on in their lives.

Apart from the benefits mentioned above, when that employee does leave, you can still maintain a healthy relationship with them and they become an external asset to you and your company. This then gives you a positive walking commercial out in the community. This positive past employee can also be someone a new prospect can talk to before joining your company. What better endorsement can you get than a positive past employee? The other option is a disgruntled ex-employee who is firing off insults and negative comments whenever they are asked about their last employment.

# Gardening

Not all of the themes above have been about dealing directly with conflict and neither is this one. This is about taking a long-term approach to how you manage people and staff. Your management style doesn't only relate to your workplace either; work and home affect each other and taking stress home from the office isn't much fun for you, your family or your friends.

I believe that managing a team at work is very similar to tending a garden over an extended period. When you come into a new team leader position, it's like moving into a new home. There's already a garden and you have the ability to grow and change it as you see fit. You can pull plants out and install new ones in your garden, the same as you can change employees, although not as easily. There is always weeding to do, which I see as conflict management in the workplace. If those weeds aren't tended to when they are small, they will continue to grow until something is done about them, or they will take over your garden.

As you can see, there are plenty of ideas to explore and unwrap further as you read through this book. I look forward to explaining more of my experiences and thoughts.

# Chapter 3

# Changing Corporate Culture from the Bottom Up

First let's talk about your current way of dealing with workplace conflict.

## What type of conflict manager are you?

Do you:

a.	Deal with all conflict by stamping your authority on it and telling others how it will be?

b.	Avoid conflict around the office and only deal with issues when they get to a serious enough level?

c.	Find out from a third party what's going on and hopefully let them sort it out themselves?

d.	Talk it through with those involved to find the solution that is the best outcome?

If you can talk through conflicts and disputes with all involved and get the best outcome for all, then well done, that's great work, and you are to be highly commended.

## How busy are you?

Unfortunately that's not how the majority of companies and managers deal with conflict. Too many people believe that they are too busy to get involved with lower level conflict, or even worse, don't notice them at all. We all have deadlines and responsibilities that we are tied to, and it's easy to punch on through with what is critical today. What I want to provide you with in this book, is a 'how to' on creating a workplace environment where people are respected and listened to. Where you can transform your workplace and deal with the issues that produce the conflict before they get 'out of hand'.

Sweeping disputes under the mat, and hoping they will 'go away' isn't a strategy that helps anyone. Disputes that are brushed aside or ignored will be talked about around the office, others will get involved, lines will be drawn, sides will be taken, and large amounts of time will be wasted. Even worse, this dispute is now a full blown conflict that will take many, extra hours to resolve.

Even if your overall corporate culture is lacking respect from you team, that doesn't mean that you and your team have to behave like that. Open communication, listening to others, hearing what they have to say, and actively welcoming new ideas will create open-minded workplaces where staff can produce positive results.

## Improve your team first

If you work on improving your team and your communication, you will be the first one to benefit. The flow-on effects from this style of management are all positive. Staff become more respectful to you and each other, retention rates improve, people enjoy being at work more, and the team reach higher achievements. The simple fact is that with fewer disputes and conflict around, the team spends more time on productive activities, and less time complaining about someone or something.

## Case Study

I worked with a company where a team leader (Karen) found it increasingly difficult to work and communicate with her manager (Warwick). The situation became progressively worse as the months went on. Warwick and Karen would argue often in his office, never seeming to be able to agree on much at all. Their conflict continued to escalate, and Karen informed Warwick's senior manager (Peter). At this point Peter didn't consider the matter serious enough for him to do anything about it.

Other team members became affected by way of discussion, and by simply viewing the growing discourse that was happening between Karen and Warwick. Everyone was growing unhappier by the day. Work standards slipped as Karen started to take days off sick. Warwick was now snapping at other staff, and the team members felt like they were left without an effective leader.

Finally Karen lodged a bullying claim against Warwick, and took 3 months extended stress leave. HR spent days working on the conflict, interviewing, evaluating, and developing a resolution. They interviewed everyone involved, Karen, Warwick, Peter, and all the team members who were affected to establish the facts.

Karen, who enjoyed working with her team, never went back to that role, and was moved to a role in a different department on her return after counselling. Her respect for senior management has declined. Mediation was offered, but rejected as Karen couldn't even be in the same room as Warwick by then. A new team leader with lesser skills was appointed as Karen's replacement, and the team's respect in him took months to establish.

Warwick was given counselling and training on his behaviour, and has become an improved manager. Warwick and the team members now get on better than at any time previously. He has quietly admitted mistakes to them, and now engages more openly and more often with them.

If only the senior manager (Peter) that Karen went to see had acted earlier, much of the stress and expense that followed would have been avoided. HR would still have been involved, but the situation may have been resolved so that Karen had kept the role she loved. The new team leader still isn't as effective as Karen was.

**Chapter 4**

# The Cost of Re-Employment

Before we get too far into the book, I want to talk about the costs of replacing a staff member. It's a natural part of business for staff to come and go in any organisation, but many of the actually costs to replace a staff member are hidden and difficult to measure.

A high staff turnover creates an extra burden on the human resources (HR) department alone. Every staffing position that needs to be re-filled requires hours of work from the HR department. Clearly, if staff turnover can be reduced, the resources needed in HR to fill those positions are also reduced.

## Staff Turnover Calculator

There is an online staff turnover cost calculator, and I want to take you through some of the hidden costs that it highlights. Please open the link now so you can plug in some figures for yourself, and see what happens.

https://au.drakeintl.com/hr-news/cost-of-turnover-calculator.aspx

First of all, enter in the obvious:

1.     The base salary of the vacant position and benefits?

2.     How long is it going to take until the vacant position is filled?


Next, the calculator helps to explore costs involving the HR department. You may not know all of the figures asked for here, but you can make an educated assumption for the exercise.


1.     What is your HR manager's hourly rate?

2.     How many hours will be spent on filling that job by those managers?

3.     What will you spend on advertising and resumé screening?

4.     How long will the interview process take?

5.     What is the cost of behavioural screenings, skills assessments and background checks?

6.     How much is spent on moving and travel expenses?

# Training

Now you have to consider training of the new employee. Whoever is training the new person will be away from their work, so you are going to need to include some of their wages in your calculation.

Productivity Ramp-up

There is also a cost of productivity ramp-up. The new person will take up to three months (or longer) to become 100% productive. During this time, either the manager or other staff will be taking time away from their duties to get the newbie 'up to speed'. Another important consideration is that the person who left took a vast wealth of Corporate Intellectual Property (CIP), and general knowledge with them. Customer and senior management relationships, past project experience and simple knowledge, like where is all the stationery kept, needs to be learned by the new appointee. The incumbent will create their own new CIP account, but information and experience take time to gather and establish. While the intellectual property of each company is confidential and usually carries severe penalties if traded, the Corporate Intellectual Property (CIP) is information that is knowledge about how the company operates. CIP is the how a company operates, and where to find information, something each employee gathers during their employment at any particular company.

# Lost Intellectual Property

I believe that the corporate IP that is lost when an employee leaves a position can create a huge drain on the company. Some companies do manage staff turnover regarding corporate knowledge well. On the other hand, there are many instances where staff leave because of their relationship with their manager and there can be very little handover. It's often not until after the employee has left that others realise just how much valuable information the person possessed. The longer the person has been in the job or with the company, the larger their CIP account is. This CIP account works differently from a normal bank account; you are always depositing into the account and increasing the balance, but when you make a withdrawal, the balance doesn't diminish. Over time, a long serving staffer can create an enormous amount of corporate intellectual property, and when that person leaves, the resource goes with them. Every new employee starts their CIP account at zero for their new company, and has to amass the information themselves. This loss of CIP can be the most hidden and difficult to value in the cost of replacing an employee. The amount of time and energy spent finding the how, where and what of issues, and contacts lost when someone with a large amount of company CIP leaves is almost unmeasurable, but it is massive.

## What is the bottom line?

I have run the numbers through this calculator several times with differing variables, and reached the conclusion that the cost of replacing a staff member is around 20 to 25% of their annual salary. The calculator is there for you to do the numbers yourself, so give it a go.

The point of this exercise is to get you thinking about the value in working at keeping staff for longer periods. I understand that people (in general), move from job to job more frequently nowadays, but that doesn't mean that all of your staff have to be a part of that trend. People move for many reasons apart from supervisor relationships, but these relationships are a significant factor for staff retention in many organisations.

Authors Marcus Buckingham and Curt Coffman said in their book, 'First Break All the Rules: What the Worlds' Greatest Managers Do Differently', that people don't leave jobs, they leave managers.

> 'If employees don't get along with their managers, don't like them or don't respect them, they will leave a company despite a high salary or great benefits. A bad manager is a big factor in employee performance. A good manager, no matter the salary, will inspire loyalty.'

What we are talking about here is creating a team culture that can inspire people to come to work. We spend so much of our time at work, why shouldn't it be a place that is enjoyable and gratifying, or at the very least worthwhile?

The cost of filling a vacant position is high, (as we have seen in this chapter), and this is what this book is about - Increasing productivity by reducing workplace conflict. The less conflict your team or department encounters, the more open the communication will become. This in turn enables higher productivity; simply because you spend more time actually doing more productive activities with people you enjoy spending time with.

# Chapter 5

# How Workplace Relationships Affect Productivity

It is well-documented that a bad boss is very high on the list of why people leave their jobs.

**People don't leave jobs**

I quoted this in the previous chapter, and I feel it is such an important point that I'm going to repeat it here. "People don't leave jobs, they leave managers." If employees don't get along with their managers, don't like them or don't respect them, they will leave a company despite a high salary or great benefits. A bad (or poor) manager is an important factor in employee performance. A good manager, no matter the salary, will inspire loyalty.

It's a very simple fact that if you don't get on well with someone at the start, that relationship probably isn't going to be great in the longer term. That's fine if it's in a social environment where you meet or get introduced to someone you don't mesh with, but if it's your boss, then you have a bit more of a problem.

## People leave managers

If it's your boss that you don't respect, you still have to turn up every day and work with them. You may be able to avoid them for a day or two, but it isn't a sustainable, rewarding relationship to have with your boss. This style of relationship is not going to produce outstanding results or high productivity and this type of relationship is more likely to increase the tension and stress levels between the two of you.

What I'm talking about here is developing a working environment where staff respect and even like their managers; the sort of respect where you can go to your manager with new concepts and ideas. A place where you know you will be listened to and heard without the fear of being brushed aside, or having your idea hijacked.

## Do unto others, as you would have them do unto you!

How you like to be treated should be how you treat your staff, so it follows that you deserve the same level of respect from your manager that you give to others. If you don't have the level of respect you deserve from your manager, then you are probably already questioning what sort of relationship you do have with them. Can you go to your boss and talk about anything; can you bring new ideas and concepts to them? If you can't, then there's work to be done on that relationship as well.

The good news is this type of relationship development can start to take place immediately. It is a long-term project that can become a natural way of working and is worth the effort, but it will take time. You don't need approval from your up-line to improve your down-line relationships. I don't know what your relationships with your staff are like now, but there is always room for improvement.

## Stand-up Coffee meetings

I want to get you thinking about how to improve your working relationships and one simple way to do this is to start having informal group meetings. They can be a stand-up coffee meeting, or any type of informal meeting, but the idea is that people feel free to talk about whatever they want to. There doesn't need be a set agenda; the idea is for it to be a relaxed environment where people are comfortable discussing any topic or challenge. These meetings only need to be 15-20 minutes at the most and they are designed to get your team more engaged in each other on a personal level.

You might find that to begin with people are mainly talking about family or sport, and what else they do outside of work. However, as time goes on, you will notice people are talking more about work, about matters that are important to them in the workplace. It is extremely important that you, as the team leader/manager attend these meetings, so that you know what's important to your staff. From this informal environment you will detect the feel of your team and pressure points that you can act on. Developing the ability to resolve these pressure points before they evolve into bigger issues will help you grow as their manager, and show staff that you are listening to and understanding them.

Notice I called them 'stand-up' coffee meetings. This is because you want people informally drifting in and out of conversations. This is an excellent opportunity for your shyer staff to feel more included too. You are creating an environment where everyone is going to feel more comfortable and more of an equal.

The timing of these meetings is up to you, however most managers I know hold them either Monday or Friday mornings. Monday morning meetings are a good start to the week with a quick catch up, and a chance to check in with everyone.  Anything that has been on your people's minds over the weekend can be brought up and discussed before heading into the week.  On the other hand, meetings at the end of the week are just as good, checking that people aren't taking baggage home into the weekend, and also celebrating any positives from the week.

# Chapter 6

# Mind Mapping and Brainstorming Conflict

As mentioned in Chapter one, mind mapping has been around for a long time, but is often discarded as 'too simple' or just something kids do at school. Both these points are true, but neither are a negative. Because it's so simple, it can be done by anyone, anywhere, anytime. The process is very easy to explain to others, and you can get down to working on a mind map within minutes. It is also true that kids use this technique at school; in fact I remember it being something my boys learned in their early years of schooling when they were about 7 or 8 years old, and they are still mind mapping for senior school subjects now.

## The basics

The concept of Mind Mapping is simply that you start with a large piece of paper and write the idea or purpose you want to explore in the middle of the page. From here the process is purely to write and link all your thoughts, ideas, connections, lists, and anything else that you think relates (even in the smallest way) to the central idea. Draw connecting lines between thoughts or ideas that relate, and soon you will have a complete overview of the whole picture.

It may not be pretty and it's not meant to be, but it will give you a global view of any issue you want to explore. Mind mapping can be used in any brainstorming situation, from simple tasks such as a junior school project, right through to high level thinking situations where you need to see all of the possibilities laid out in one place. I used mind mapping to lay out my overall concept for this book, and then a separate one for every chapter in the book. Without this simple tool and process, this book would have taken me much, much longer to write, or may not have been published at all. So I know the process works.

## Important

Mind mapping isn't something you should try to do on a computer - it must be physically written on a piece of paper. Trying to do this on a computer doesn't give you the same visual effect and isn't as stimulating. The great advantage of a Mind Map is that it literally "maps" the way your brain sees and creates connections. It brings incredible clarity and ease to any decision-making process, using all of the ways your brain processes information - word, image, logic and spatial awareness, so that you are literally thinking with your whole brain.

Other benefits of mind mapping include:

    A.    Easy recall and being able to see all of the information in the one place

Being able to show others how different parts of an issue connect and relate

    B.    Continual brainstorming, drawing other people's ideas and perceptions into the map

    C.    Transforming a complicated situation into simple, actionable tasks

I have also used mind mapping in individual conflict circumstances and I suggest you use it for mapping conflict within your team.

It's a very simple 3 step process:

    a.    Mind Map

    b.    Outline

    c.    Schedule

### a. Mind map

The mind map itself is the first of 3 steps to put your workplace conflict into perspective, and to prioritise your tasks.

Give yourself at least half an hour of undisturbed time for this mind mapping exercise. Turn off your phone, stay away from your computer, emails and any other distractions that will break your concentration during this time. When all you are focusing on is the mind map, 30 minutes will produce an amazing road map for you to use in the next step – the outline.

Remember this is a brain dump; list everything you can think of about your workplace conflict.

a. Facts

b. Concepts

c. Ideas

d. Names

e. Lists

f. Events

g. Phrases

h. the ridiculous; and

i. the important

Just keep writing as your mind focuses on different aspects of your conflict. Don't worry about structure or spelling, just produce and record all your ideas on any sort of conflict happening around your workplace. Include large and smaller events. Keep going for 30 minutes and write every detail you can remember; order isn't important at this stage, it's all about getting your thoughts down on paper.

At the end of 30 minutes you will have an amazing piece of work detailing your team's workplace conflict. It may look like a bit of a mess at this stage, with lines drawn all over the page connecting ideas, lists, thoughts and concepts. Don't worry; it should look like a bit of a mess. As your mind begins to connect items, you can see the whole big picture on one page, and start constructive work from here.

I believe this mind mapping process is one of the most under-utilised tools in management today. The way it brings all of the ideas together and lays it out on one page (or whiteboard) for everyone to see is extremely powerful. It enables you to explain to others how pieces are connected where they had had difficulty seeing the connection before. It clarifies those thoughts in your mind that have been bouncing around, and possibly even giving you sleepless nights.

Now you can move onto the next stage.

## b. Outline

# How to turn your jumbled thoughts into an easy to follow outline

This step in the brainstorming process is to make sense of the mind map you have created, and put structure into the planning. By studying your jumbled, mixed up mind map, you will already have noticed that there are pieces which fit together and themes that stand out, which have a number of sub-sections to them.

Now by working with those major themes, you will dissect and rearrange your mind map into a sequenced, actionable, solid plan. At this stage it still doesn't have to be perfect, and you could continue working on the detail forever, but your jumbled mess is beginning to take shape and have structure.

So, what are the major themes from your brain dump? You might find you have 5 or 7, or even more strong themes. It doesn't really matter how many you have. The important action now is to gather the remaining points from the map and organise them under these themes. You may have recurring issues that have come up, or people who appear in numerous places. Some conflicts will have been expected, and you will realise new conflicts or see new ways of looking at old issues. When this is true its good news. It means that the mind map has got your brain thinking differently, and re-framed the subject so that you are considering it from a new angle.

This is becoming your guide to move forward, setting you up to be able to tackle the issues you have identified. At some point in the process you will want to start thinking about sharing this information with others. This may be your immediate manager, mentor, peers, or people within your team. They may even be outside of your workplace. But please think carefully about whom you share this information with; people within your team may not be the first you should share with. Some people can get their noses out of joint pretty easily, so be mindful of how you relay the information to those that report to you. You are in the process of creating an improved working environment, not a more uncomfortable one. Confidentiality is also a consideration at all times, so be mindful of who you divulge any information to.

I suggest you talk through what you have discovered so far with your immediate manager or mentor. You may consider bringing them into the process earlier and involve them right from the start, but that's up to you. Your manager should be pleased to see you on the front foot, tackling conflict as an important part of your role. That's up to you and depends on your actual relationship with your manager, but hopefully they notice that you're up to something. From here the next step is to schedule items for action.

## c.  Schedule

## Turning your outline into actionable events

This is where you get into the detail.  You have the map, you've made the outline, so now is the time to schedule yourself a timeline and plot events that will see you achieve solid milestones.  The planning you complete in this area will provide you with the structure to change culture, mould your team, and set your leadership style.  Prioritise your themes, and start working towards how and when you will act on them.  You've done all the hard work to get to this point, and this is where it all comes together.  You should be starting to feel more comfortable with undertaking some of the tasks you are setting for yourself.  The more you prepare, the better the outcome will be.

There will still be difficult conversations to have, and this may produce uncomfortable realisations for some.  The sooner you have these conversations though, the sooner everyone can work towards a better future.  Sweeping issues under the carpet and ignoring them is no good for anyone.  It's time to get real and deal with the issues you have uncovered.  You should be able to ask your up-line for help where you feel you need it, but managers want you to bring suggested solutions into discussions – not just problems.

It is prudent to have a third party present when having difficult conversations for a number of reasons.  This person should be someone you both feel comfortable with, and you will need to explain why there is another person involved. Explain that the third party is a witness for both of you and is present to substantiate details of the conversation if necessary. If the conversation gets heated, the third party can be called upon to describe what they saw happen. This can also avoid arguments over what took place during the discussion and can moderate the conversation during proceedings to avoid increasing tensions. You can also allow the person you are having the difficult conversation with to bring a support person with them for similar reasons.

Be prepared to defend your actions in these difficult conversations, as not everyone will want to hear what you have to say.

# Case Study

I recall this situation where the conversation didn't end as the manager had planned. The manager had the difficult conversation with the staff member alone, and was subsequently reported to HR for bullying. This then took much longer to attempt to resolve, entangled many more people, and as a result, the staff member left the company disgruntled and disillusioned. This wasn't the outcome the manager was after at all. It started with a relatively small issue that needed to be resolved, and as a result of holding the conversation in the wrong environment, the company lost a valued team member through poor management. The manager involved consequently required counselling as his stress levels had escalated, and was given extra training to strengthen his inadequate skills in this area. It would have been much better if this training had been provided to the manager before the incident occurred.

## Recurring Issues

You may also have identified a few recurring conflicts in the mind mapping process, issues that come up periodically, but aren't getting addressed or solved. Often these conflicts are smaller in nature, and one way or another these 'issues' get brushed aside, or people 'make do' with the system they have and work around the problem. The trouble with this type of unresolved conflict is that it provides an underlying belief that 'some things never change', 'it's too hard to fix the problem', or 'that's just the way it is around here'. Now we are talking about the culture of your company, and how your actual company culture exists in your staff's minds. What is the difference between your corporate definition of your culture, and what is happening day to day 'on the ground' in your team?

The corporate (induction manual) definition of your company culture might sound great (or not), but your actual culture is how people relate and communicate with each other, each and every day.

So what is your team's culture? Is it something you are proud of?

## Big Picture Stuff

We are starting to talk about big picture stuff now, so I just want to point out that you are not going to change your entire company culture simply by making one mind map. It is however, an excellent place to start. From a workplace conflict mind map, you can see how big your challenge is, and how much work there it to do. So take a deep breath, start with the smaller conflict issues, and work your way up. This is an achievable goal.

On your timeline, plot out simpler tasks sooner, and the more complex issues further down the track. Rocket science I know, but the experience and confidence you gain from dealing and solving the smaller jobs will inspire you to tackle the bigger ones. Knocking off some smaller tasks early will also show others that you are working on their concerns, and that in turn will give your team more confidence in you.

That's enough on mind mapping for now. Plenty more will come out of the work you do around this, and remember, if you get stuck on any problem or conflict, a mind map is a great way to lay all the facts out in a simple format.

# Chapter 7

# Dealing with Difficult People

## Where do they come from?

Who are these people? They weren't like that when you hired them, or you wouldn't have hired them in the first place. I see two possibilities here - either the person was very good at hiding their true personality when you hired them, or something has changed in them over time. People are constantly encountering concerns and challenges both inside and outside of work, which can add extra pressure to their lives and make them more difficult to deal with.

There are also people who are moved into your team from other departments that come with a history or reputation for being difficult. Whichever way these difficult people have arrived into your team, you now have to deal with them, and it could be driving you crazy. Here is a good example of the 80/20 rule which you have probably familiar with. In this case, 20% (or less) of the people are causing you 80% of the headaches. They may be very good at getting the job done, but the way they go about it makes the rest of the team uncomfortable and unsettled.

## Personality Conflicts

Personality conflict at work can be a difficult area to manage because of the very nature of people. This is where a great manager stands out. They are the ones who are able to manage the different personalities within their team to get the best out of the unit. In every team you will have all manner of personalities to deal with, from the introvert to the extrovert, and many levels in between. I've said it before and I'll say it again; "People don't leave jobs, they leave managers". When you can deal with or learn to deal with these difficult people, you become more valued to your managers, as well as accomplishing more with your own team.

A good manager, no matter the salary, will inspire loyalty. Loyalty inspires trust, which in turn leads to increased staff retention, which leads to higher productivity.

# Cycle of High Conflict Thinking

Before I go any further I want to provide you with a simple analogy of the cycle of high conflict thinking. This explanation comes from Bill Eddy, a very well respected international speaker, mediator and lawyer.

1. <u>MAD</u>  Mistaken Assessment of Danger

2. <u>BAD</u>  Behaviour that's Aggressively Defensive

3. <u>N.F.</u>  Negative Feedback

By starting at the MAD sector (1), someone mistakes their situation as under threat and sees that as a danger to them and their position. From there they become aggressively defensive or BAD (2). When that happens and they receive negative feedback (3), the high conflict thinker cycles back to MAD (1) and the cycle repeats.

Although this is a simple cycle, you can see how over time people in the cycle become accustomed to believing that everyone and everything is against them, and out to get them. This can be a very difficult cycle to break, especially if it has been their default behaviour for a long time. Unfortunately, people in this cycle don't often see themselves as the problem. It's always someone else's fault, and because their aggressive behaviour often gets them what they want, this purely reinforces the behaviour.

You can find more information on this topic and Bill Eddy at http://www.highconflictinstitute.com/, or my website http://www.mimmediation.net

## My Lifeline experience

As I mentioned earlier in the book, I have been volunteering and working with Lifeline Melbourne for a few years now. One of the many things I've learned talking to people on the phone, is that people want to be listened to. They want to have the time to tell their story and to be heard. I understand that everyone is busy and time is precious at work, however to reduce conflict in the workplace you are going to need to take the time to listen to people.

Whether or not your company has a scheduled one-on-one staff evaluation program with your team members, you should include these as part of your management strategy. Most large companies have regular official appraisal sessions 2 or 3 times a year. While they are great for keeping everything 'on record' and ticking all the boxes, some people see them as a waste of time and that nothing ever comes out of them. Make yours worthwhile; they can be a natural extension of the 'stand-up coffee' meetings described in chapter 5. If you are having regular conversations with your team members, and you both feel comfortable talking about issues that are affecting you, when you get to the official appraisal, there shouldn't be any surprises for either party.

This isn't to say this will come easy to you, or that it's your natural style, but it sure beats hiding away, pretending everything is going along fine and then coming in heavy handed at the official appraisal. I hope that's not your current management style, and if it is, I wonder how well that's working for you?

## What's their real beef?

Why are these difficult people so difficult? Often there is something else going on well outside of your control and maybe outside of their control as well. It could be their family, grief, loneliness, a mental illness, or any number of other influences that is causing them to act inappropriately at work, and therefore coming across as 'difficult'. On the other hand, they may not realise how they appear to others, it is just their natural way of operating. Either way, as a member of your team, you have to deal with them.

# Reflection doesn't help with high conflict people

Those who live in this state of high conflict don't react well to having their poor past performance pointed out to them. They tend to have a justification or excuse for how they acted in the past, and convincing them to see their past mistakes is usually a waste of time for all involved. You end up getting frustrated, and the difficult party is headed for their comfort zone again – the cycle of high conflict thinking.

A healthier approach is to forward focus them, but you need to ensure that you have connected with them first. This is another Lifeline principle; others won't open up to you if you don't have empathy, listen, and respect them first. You need to spend some time listening and getting to understand why they are like they are. What is it about this particular event that is upsetting them? Focus them on the particular event that has brought you to this discussion, and bring them back to that event if they bring other matters into the conversation. These high conflict people are experts at bringing in 'red herrings' to distract the conversation away from the point in contention. By building empathy with them, you gain more respect and allow them to talk more freely, where you can find underlying issues.

## What to do with underlying issues?

Often the underlying issue is completely different from the conflict of the moment, but when you are able to find that underlying issue and work with them on that, it can be your best and most rewarding work. By seeking and finding their underlying challenges, you can start to heal long time wounds, which over time can improve relationships in many areas of their lives.

Once you have some understanding of the deeper issues for the difficult, high conflict person, you can work on future performance. While you cannot change the past, you can plan for better interactions in the future. These people may not even see their past communications as a problem (especially for them), so highlighting a specific past interaction isn't worth the effort. Instead, spend time and energy in working with them on how to achieve better outcomes in the future.

## Listening for invitations

Offer options and suggestions while working with them, but the solutions need to come from them. You need to be listening for phrasing and invitations that indicate that they are ready to approach the future with a more positive outlook. When you hear a positive change from them, give encouragement so that it can grow into a more constructive idea which you can develop further together.

Again, I must acknowledge that this may not be comfortable work, and it won't be all plain sailing (some people are very stuck in their ways), but this is about changing behaviour over a prolonged period.

This is a much larger topic than I can cover in this book, so if these discussions and work interests you, or you have more questions on anything discussed so far, please contact me at

www.mimmediation.net or malguy@mimmediation.net

If you can adopt at least some of the tools prescribed so far in this book, people around you will notice the positive effect you are having on your team, and on others. By maintaining your effort through the smaller actions like 'stand-up coffee' meetings, and being willing to listen to other peoples challenges, you will be amazed at how your team culture can be improved. As we know, "from little things, big things grow". By setting yourself an achievable timeline to accomplish reasonable goals, productivity will improve. You are now fostering a more comfortable working environment by reducing workplace conflict. This isn't something you can perfect overnight, but it can be achieved through consistent behaviour on your part, and by setting your environment to foster this change.

Be the change you want to see in others.

# Chapter 8

# Bullying and How to Maintain a Reliable Workplace Policy

## BULLYING IS DISCRIMINATION, BUT DOES NOT DISCRIMINATE

### A quick overview

Bullying is a very important issue for all concerned. Whether you are the one being bullied, the one doing the bullying, or the manager of a team where bullying is happening, there are ramifications for all when this type of activity occurs in your workplace.

If you feel you are being bullied or believe anyone else is, in any situation, you should seek help. If you don't know where to start, or if you're unsure if what you are experiencing is bullying, here are a few places to begin:

## Resources and help lines

International web search for bullying information, help and links to individual countries

www.befrienders.org/bullying-at-work

Lifeline (Australia)

www.lifeline.org.au          13 11 14

Beyond Blue

www.beyondblue.org.au

Suicide Callback Service        (Australia)

www.suicidecallbackservice.org.au   13 659 467

Suicide prevention lifeline (USA)

www.suicidepreventionlifeline.org/GetHelp  1-800-273-TALK (8255)

Bullying helpline (UK)
http://www.nationalbullyinghelpline.co.uk/ Tel: 0845 22 55 787

The important thing is to seek help and talk to others about your experience.

## An Internationally Recognised Problem

DAVID CAMERON (UK):

"Stamping out bullying in the workplace and elsewhere is a vital objective. Not only can bullying make people's lives a misery, but it harms business and wider society too."

Bullying can damage a person's health and self-esteem, affecting their happiness and performance both inside and outside the workplace.

LADY GAGA:

"I've been actually really very pleased to see how much awareness was raised around bullying, and how deeply it affects everyone. You know, you don't have to be the loser kid in high school to be bullied. Bullying and being picked on comes in so many different forms."

## Around the world

Bullying is a huge issue around the world today, no more so than in the workplace. Bullying, its implications in the workplace and to productivity are well documented. I believe that to cover the subject respectfully I would need to write a separate book entirely on the subject. Please keep reading, but for more information and assistance around bullying at work, please contact me at www.mimmediation.net or malguy@mimmediation.net

Some countries have clearly defined government legislation on bullying, Australia being one of them. In Australia on January 1st 2014, federal legislation came into effect so that all states and territories now operate under the same umbrella of The Fair Work Commission. This is a welcome step forward from a few years ago when different states and territories of the country operated under different legislation. At least now the legal process is uniform across the country.

# Brodie's Law

In September 2006, 19-year-old Brodie Panlock suicided after enduring ongoing humiliating and intimidating bullying by her co-workers at a café in Melbourne, Australia.

The tragedy of Brodie's death was compounded by the fact that none of those responsible for bullying Brodie were charged with a serious criminal offence. Instead, each offender was convicted and fined under the State Occupational Health and Safety Act.

Brodie's death was a tragic example of the severe consequences that bullying can have on victims, their families and the community. This clearly illustrates that at the time, there were obvious constraints in the law. Following Brodie's suicide, her parents and friends worked extremely hard for several years to change the law in Victoria.

In 2011 after 5 long years, Victoria introduced anti-bullying legislation known as Brodie's Law, and made serious bullying a crime punishable by up to 10 years jail.

Brodie's case is extreme, but it tragically highlights the fact that bullying can have life-threatening implications that others do not see. While nobody can know exactly what it was like for Brodie, we know what she experienced drove her to take her life. I cannot imagine what that was like for her, but I do know that no-one should experience that level of harassment or distress at work.

To learn more about Brodie's Law and how it changed legislation in Australia go to:
http://www.justice.vic.gov.au/home/safer+communities/crime+prevention/bullying+-+brodies+law#breadcrumbs

## Your Responsibilities

As a manager you have a serious obligation to ensure that bullying is dealt with according to the law and company policy. As a human being, morally you should be looking out for your work colleagues and helping those who need support.

## Establishing clear policy and procedures

You need to have boundaries firmly established so that everyone knows where they stand. Ensure you (as the leader) and your entire team know your company policy in this area, and know where to find it if anyone asks. It is not good enough to say you have a policy; everyone must know what it is and where to find it at a moment's notice.

# Definition of Workplace Bullying

The Fair Work Commission's Anti-bullying Benchbook defines bullying as follows:

"Workplace bullying occurs when:

An individual or group of individuals repeatedly behaves unreasonably towards a worker or a group of workers at work,

AND

The behaviour creates a risk to health and safety.

Reasonable management action conducted in a reasonable manner does not constitute workplace bullying."

If you don't know or don't understand your company policy, now is the time to find out. This is not something to put off until tomorrow, ensure you are clear on your company policy now. Talk with HR about your actual procedure, go through the steps with them, and understand the implications for everyone.

# Effects of bullying

## On the one being bullied

The effects of workplace bullying can be far reaching and have very serious negative consequences on the health and wellbeing of your staff. The individuals involved may develop depression, anxiety, nausea, or other health issues. They may experience trouble sleeping and need time off work through stress leave. As we have seen above in Brodie's experience, the consequences can be extreme.

## On the bully

These people also need help. For whatever reason, they are acting inappropriately and could lose their job over their bullying actions. There are possibly underlying issues that a bully needs to address, apart from the obvious bullying action that is happening. The bully may not want to address these underlying issues, which then complicates the situation by making it more involved, requiring ongoing discussions and counselling.

The bullying needs to be dealt with as per company policy and procedures, again remembering that this is taking many, many hours, and staff members away from the team's primary objectives.

# On your team

Bullying has a huge impact on some companies and can cost them lost productivity in many areas. Along with the person who is being bullied, others in the team will be affected. Some staff will take sides and feel emotions similar to the victim or perpetrator. At the very least, many hours of productive time get lost through the actions of a bully. The work needed to get everyone back on track is considerable, and will involve HR, senior management, and possibly professional outside support as well.

Productivity takes a huge hit. As staff share their thoughts on the situation, left uncontrolled, a bullying episode can run like wild-fire through an organisation. One bullying experience can seriously undermine team morale, confidence and culture, that you have spent an extended period cultivating. Staff may need to be moved between departments, or need to be replaced altogether, taking resources from your bottom line.

All in all, you don't want bullying happening in your team, on your watch. Thankfully, if you are observant and know your team well, you will notice if a bully is at work amongst your team. It is important that the rest of your team feel comfortable in knowing that if they suspect a bully is at work, they can come and talk to you about it. When you act on this information early and take the correct steps, you will stay in control of the situation and your team.

Failure to act will only worsen the event and be detrimental to your staff and team overall. Apart from the possibly severe and harmful mental health impact on individuals, overall team productivity suffers as well.

## On the company

For a company, bullying can be like a cancer, with others feeding off the perceived acceptance of one or more individuals. If this bullying cancer is displayed by senior management, then company culture will be influenced, enhancing the impression in the organisation that bullying is acceptable. This can be a serious and difficult tumour to remove from a workplace.

If senior management don't take bullying seriously, or are part of the problem, then it will only be a matter of time until the company is in court over it. Unfortunately for the ones being bullied, court proceedings are never a pleasant experience. Being dragged through the prolonged legal process, having the details brought up again and again after having gone through the whole bullying drama in the first place, can only be detrimental to their mental health.

Aside from the internal conflict, distress, and lost productivity for the company, the brand damage to the business once customers and the wider public are aware of a bullying culture can be extreme. Once a company is perceived to have a bullying culture, it can take a lot of spin and effort to reclaim lost trust and market share. Losing market share to competitors is one thing, but to lose it because of a bullying culture is another experience altogether. To have to rebuild positive brand awareness after the public perceives you as having a bullying culture, could be one of the most costly and unnecessary media campaigns your company ever runs.

## So how important is it to you?

As the leader of your team no matter how large or small, you owe it to yourself, your team members and your superiors to always be on the lookout for bullying behaviour. The sooner any bullying is identified and stopped, the better for everyone.

From the unfortunate person being bullied, right through to the shareholder, nobody likes a bully.

## One last thing on bullying

People don't appreciate being told; "I know how you feel". You can imagine how others feel, but it's impossible to 'know' how someone else feels.

You are not them!

## **Welcome to my life**

"No, you don't know what it's like
When nothing feels all right
You don't know what it's like
To be like me
To be hurt
To feel lost
To be left out in the dark
To be kicked when you're down
To feel like you've been pushed around
To be on the edge of breaking down
And no one's there to save you
No, you don't know what it's like

Welcome to my life"

Lyrics by Simple Plan, a Canadian Rock Band

# Chapter 9

# Dealing with Recurring Conflict Issues

## Why don't they get fixed and what to do about it?

These little gems of conflict are the ones that just keep on giving. You think you've fixed them in the past (maybe many times), but they'll come around again soon enough, wasting your time and clogging up your in-box. You're never going to stop all of these recurring conflicts, but you can slow down the rate of occurrence of some, and eliminate others.

## Why don't these problems get fixed?

There are actually not many reasons these recurring problems don't get fixed. It's usually either:

1.   A process

2.   A policy or;

3.   A person

All of these can be dealt with given the time and the resources. Processes can be modified, policies can be amended, and people can be transformed. Some will take much more work than others, but when you are dedicated to your task you will find a way to work through the challenges. Certainly you will need help, but you are working towards improving productivity and your team, so it is worth the effort. The other point to remember is that you aren't working in isolation, you are part of a bigger team and there are other people around to help and support you. Don't be afraid to ask for help, but also don't be put off by negative comments from those who have tried before and failed.

## Control what you can.

We need to go back to mind mapping now, have another look at your original mind map and see what stands out to you as your recurring issues. The trick here is to notice whether the same issue is arising for or from different people, in or outside of your team. Work out if it is a process, a policy or a person that is the problem. What is causing that bottleneck that hasn't been addressed?

Whatever the issue is, it's probably been challenged in the past, and for numerous reasons, the issue is still there. It can lay dormant for months at a time, only to reappear as a long forgotten enemy, once again drawing you into an unwanted, unresolved battle.

## A mini mind map

I suggest this is a perfect opportunity for another (mini) 'mind map'. This time you are going to drill down into this particular recurring conflict. See what has been attempted before, why it hasn't worked, who has been involved, and anything else you can unpack on the topic. Firstly, draw on all of your knowledge about this conflict and lay it out on the mind map to see what stands out.

I have a plan to help you work through this process so that you don't get bogged down and spend too much time on it.

It's very simple, but when followed, complicated issues become clear very quickly.

I believe when you set a defined timeframe you achieve an outcome. However, by allowing more time for the same task, you will fill up the extra time, with very few extra benefits. I know this has worked for me in the past. When I was writing this book I set some pretty tight timeframes, and I was surprised by how quickly it all came together, simply by setting these timeframes (deadlines) in the first place. OK, you're not writing a book, so the timeframe for making your mini mind map is much shorter and here it is:

## 1.    Mind Map

> Spend 12 minutes on this mind map, yep, just 12 minutes. Start by writing the recurring issue in the middle of the page and then write down everything you know about the problem. It's the same process as described in the earlier chapter, but in a shorter timeframe. If you can see a pattern of the recurrence, then write down the steps in that pattern. Include people, departments, places; anything that comes to mind in these 12 minutes.

## 2. Outline

Spend the next 12 minutes analysing your mind map. Again it's only 12 minutes, but that is enough time for you to develop an outline to further flesh out your action plan. This is almost identical to step 2 in the mind map I explained earlier in this book, I simply want to go over it again here as a refresher. From the mind map break it down into sections. Go through the mind map, find the ideas and themes that go together, and then group them into your 'sections'. These sections will help you to lay down the foundations of where everything sits at the moment, what has been attempted to resolve the issue in the past, and hopefully why some of those previous attempts didn't work. Don't be constrained by my suggestions though, you may come up with several more sections or themes from your mind map, so go with what is right for you. This is your issue you are working on, so you need to be comfortable with the plan you are developing.

## 3. Timeline

Next, bring the mind map and outline into a useable timeline that will provide stepping stones for you to progress through to the resolution of your issue.

You will have started to see how things flow from section to section in step 2, and by now you will have a pretty good idea of what has happened in the past, and what you need to do to stop the issue from returning again and again in the future. You may need extra resources in the form of specialised people to complete some of the tasks. For instance, if you need to implement amendments to policies, you will need input from a number of departments which will take longer to achieve than other parts of your timeline.

The important point is to write out your timeline and keep it in a visible place so you don't lose momentum. Make your timeline realistic, but not too drawn out. You know best how your company operates, and how long some matters can take to change.

Make people accountable to you. Get people to agree to an actual deadline date in an email with the actions required. Check in with them before the deadline is due, gently reminding them of your expectations. This is a much more engaging management style, to be questioning and helping along the way, rather than yelling and screaming after the deadline has past.

## 4. Review with peers

As we have discussed above, some of this is going to take a while, so it's important to engage others in the process. If you're changing policy and procedure then this is obviously an involved process, and even if you're undertaking a simpler change, you will need to involve others. You are already well prepared for this by having developed your mind map, outline and timetable. You can present all of these resources to your manager and/or peers, knowing that you can answer any queries and questions they throw at you with confidence.

Some of these managers will have more input, and this can be a great time to create a new mind map with them. Explain the mind map process as I have and tell them that it needs to be completed quickly. If they simply help in the mind mapping stage, you can complete the outline and timetable afterwards to present to them at the next meeting, or by email. By getting them to help develop the mind map, they are 'buying into' the process, and will be much more likely to help you remove barriers where they can.

Again I remind you that this is a process, and you need to be in it for the long haul; you might upset some people, both in your team and outside of it. You will need to be strong and be ready for resistance from these people, but stay resilient in the knowledge that what you are doing is worth it. You are creating a better working environment for you and your team. Your job will become less complicated because you are reducing the amount of conflict around you. When you reduce conflict, you can enjoy coming to work more. It sounds a bit clichéd I know, but these tips I'm giving you here will have a snowball effect on you and the people around you.

## Getting senior managers on-side

I briefly touched on getting other managers to help in the mind mapping process in step 4 above. I want to expand on that a little here, as it is worthwhile explaining the benefits of getting your peers and senior managers involved in this process.

It may be that some of these senior managers have attempted to solve this very problem in the past and failed. If this is the case, you want them to be helping you by being involved in this process. If they feel on the outer, or that they haven't been consulted, they may consciously or unconsciously slow down any improvements you are attempting to implement, or even sabotage your efforts.

By getting these 'people of influence' to understand and work with you, you can remove some of the barriers that might block your progress. Apart from that great assistance, you create a multiplying effect because their influence will affect others, and this in turn can propel you even further.

I cannot state the importance of this fact enough. Making sure these 'people of influence' in your company know what you are doing and ensuring that they are kept up to date, will have a huge impact on the progress of your work. You don't necessarily need to take up a lot of their time; you simply need to keep them in the loop. These 'people of influence' can be incredible allies when they are working with you, but be aware of the destructive impact they can assert when you upset them, it can be crushing.

## Fixing recurring conflicts is like creating passive income

Imagine the feeling knowing that you have been instrumental in solving a problem that has been draining the company for years. The knowledge that it was you who started the process, and kept it going when things got tough, is a huge reward in itself. Sure, you will have had help from others, but it was your energy that propelled and continued the process. It's ok to give yourself some credit, you deserve it. You've probably been dealing with company politics along the way and interacting with people outside your comfort zone. All of that can be very draining, but the knowledge that you have dealt with this issue is not the only reward.

Albert Einstein is quoted as saying, "Insanity is doing the same thing over and over again and expecting different results".  Not fixing these recurring conflicts within a company is therefore a type of insanity.  I see these recurring conflicts as a tremendous drain on a company in lost time alone, and then there is the lowering of staff morale that follows.  Simply having to deal with the same issue and related problems again and again is enough to drive some people crazy, and others to simply leave the company.

## Important tip

By removing, or at least reducing conflict from the company, you have increased productivity by freeing up time that would have been spent dealing with it in the future.  This is what I am calling 'hidden passive income'.  You don't notice when the event is not happening, but if you hadn't fixed it, the costs would still be there.

One of the vexing aspects of what I am saying is that when it works and there is less conflict, people don't always notice.  People seldom notice what isn't there, so when there is no conflict; people are correct in assuming that is how interactions are supposed to happen.  Just as it was when there was conflict, most people simply accepted that.

Part of the joy in teaching this process and system is that is does make a difference, even though not everyone will notice. In your team, because you are starting the change, you get to notice and enjoy it more. It's a great thing to be able to change a team's culture, but it does take time and effort, and it is something that you should be very proud of. As you continue on your journey and you continue to modify your management style, you will become more confident in using these tools. The tools become the natural way of interacting with your team and management, and soon enough it will become your natural management style.

Hopefully you will see positive changes in your private life too, with both family and friends. It starts with you, but the tools you learn and use from this book will have a positive impact on many others around you, simply by how you model yourself.

# Chapter 10

# The Conflict Continuum

# Hidden Costs of Avoidance and Wasted Time in Conflict

In this chapter we are discussing the effects of the cost of avoidance, and what spiralling into more confrontational conflict involves. Be aware that I'm not just talking about the monetary cost. While there is obviously a bottom line cost to avoidance, the costs also involve damage to brand image, losing control of the outcome, time and stress.

The conflict continuum is my way of expressing how a simple grievance can grow and intensify all the way up to war if left unchecked. All conflict, including wars, started with a small disagreement or misunderstanding.

Just so we are clear here, when I talk about any of the terms below, I do so on the understanding that this is a fluid continuum and the issue at hand can move along it, stop, or jump ahead at any time during the conflict. (The dispute can also de-escalate and move down the continuum, which is what we would all hope for). Whether I'm discussing a grievance, complaint, dispute or conflict, the concepts are generally the same. The difference is usually the time frame and individuals' perception of the issue at hand.

## The Conflict Continuum

Where do your disagreements sit on the conflict continuum?

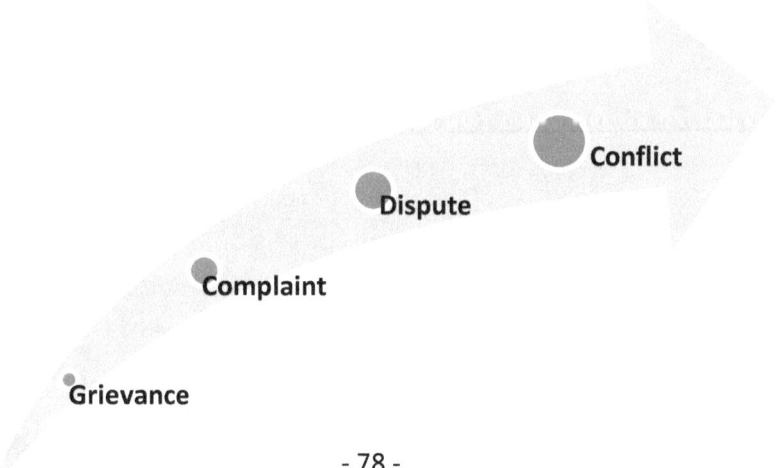

Dealing with disputes can be complicated by a lack of understanding about the basics of complaints and disputes, so here is a simple explanation of the phases of the conflict continuum. From here you can explore your disputes and see how far along the continuum you actually are.

a.     A grievance is a real or imagined cause to complain, especially related to a feeling of resentment over something believed to be wrong or unfair.

b.     A complaint is a written or verbal statement that something is unsatisfactory or unacceptable.

c.     A dispute is a disagreement or argument.

d.     A conflict is a serious disagreement or argument, typically a protracted one.

Different organisations use language in different ways, so please interpret the language and terms I use here in a way that is meaningful to your organisation.

## The Dispute Resolution Continuum

While I was conducting research for this book, I came across a blog from Lorene Schaefer where she described and posted the following chart. I was already aware of the concept Lorene discussed in her blog, but this is the best and simplest way I have seen it displayed. Rather than attempt to recreate the chart myself, I have obtained permission from Lorene to use the chart here.

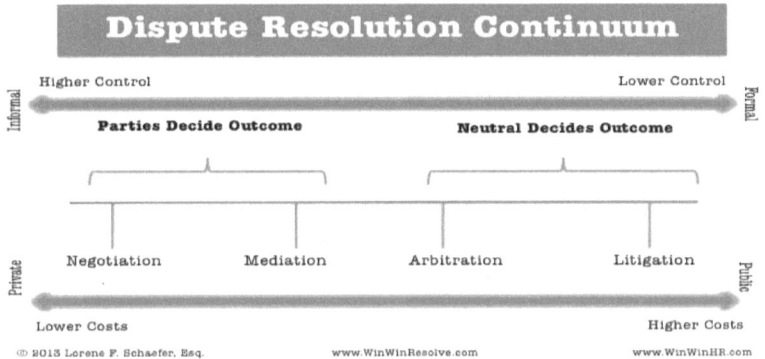

Lorene's chart makes it clear to see how disputes change, depending on how you deal with a disagreement. As you move left to right, from negotiation to litigation, many contributing influences evolve along the way, as we will discuss.

Thanks again to Lorene and her blog. To enquire further about her work and company, Win Win HR; check out the website at www.winwinhr.com/. Lorene is also President of Workplace Group USA, LLC, and you can find out more about the good work she is doing there at www.workplacegroupusa.com

# Definitions of the common dispute resolution terms

Before we discuss the chart in detail, I want to ensure that you understand the terms we are discussing.

## Negotiation

When you are in negotiation, you and the other parties discuss directly the conflict and attempt to work it out between yourselves. This is the most cost effective and productive solution, and is what happens in most cases. This is typically how most civilisations and organisations function and evolve.

## Mediation

When you are in mediation, the parties in conflict agree for a third-party neutral person (the mediator), to work with them to help and support them to resolve their conflict. The mediator is impartial and does not 'pass judgment'. Instead, the mediator's role is to manage and direct the process in the best possible way to bring the parties together, and have them find their own solution. A mediator may clarify and highlight issues to assist the parties in understanding the other's point of view. A mediator will ensure that all parties have the opportunity to explain themselves in their own words and be heard. Another important aspect of mediation is that people must listen to how others are feeling, and understand what that is like for them. Although a mediator may point out potential strengths and weaknesses, the final decisions and outcomes always lie with the participants in the conflict. Mediation may also involve private sessions with the individual parties, and can be conducted remotely over the internet or by phone.

## Arbitration

In arbitration, the parties involved in the conflict agree to a third-party (the arbitrator), to hear the evidence from each of the parties, and then the arbitrator decides on the outcome. The arbitrator's decision can either be binding or non-binding to the parties, depending on the terms of the agreement set out before the actual arbitration starts. While arbitration still allows for people to tell their stories and be heard, they have now given the decision making power to someone outside the conflict. Arbitration is very similar to mediation in most ways, but the fact that a third-party is deciding the outcome is a significant change.

# Litigation

Once you are in litigation you are heading towards court. The term litigation is used to describe the filing of a lawsuit in court, and the process that follows the filing of the lawsuit. In the simplest terms, this is going to cost you more (in time and money), and you will have even less control over the outcome. You may not even get to put your side of the case to the judge as it will probably be conducted through your lawyer. If you don't like the decision the judge hands down, apart from heading to a higher court, you are stuck with it.

## Who is in control?

Who is in control of the outcome changes dramatically as you head towards the right of the chart, and really, who wants to let someone else tell you how to resolve your conflict? Keeping control of the outcome can make the whole process much more bearable in the long run. At the end of any conflict resolution you have to live with the outcome, and the more control you have along the way, the more likely you will be able to move on afterwards. The whole concept of going through any of the processes in the continuum is to be able to put the past behind you, and close that chapter for good.

## Be a part of the solution

It is so much more powerful for you to be a part of the solution. Apart from any other costs, solving the issues at hand earlier should give you more 'peace of mind'. The negotiation and mediation processes are designed to allow you the best opportunities to be a part of the solution, and it's in your best interests to make the most of those opportunities. There are always exceptions to any rule, but in my humble opinion, I believe mediation in particular to be an excellent tool for resolving almost any conflict.

## Keeping things private and less formal

For a company, keeping conflicts 'in-house' is important, and again as you move to the right, more and more people will become aware of your 'dirty laundry' (so to speak).

The cost to your brand through negative comments on media platforms can see brand damage escalate very quickly these days. Whether it's social or mainstream media, once people are publicly commenting on your brand in a negative fashion, this can snowball very quickly and be extremely difficult and costly to control and claw back. If you can keep your disputes out of the public arena, you can save yourself a lot of time and energy.

While any conflict resolution can be distressing, the further to the right of both of the continuums, the more formal and litigious proceedings become. Again, the earlier the process of resolution (healing) can begin, the less stress will be added. Remember, everyone involved will already be under a lot of stress, and heading to court will only add to those stress levels.

Something else to consider is the length of time involved in these processes. While mediation and arbitration can be lengthy, heading for the courts and litigation usually involves a much longer time frame. Any time extension in these processes such as litigation stops you from moving on, and can add to already heightened stress levels.

Choosing whether to go to court or to resolve the dispute earlier is in your hands. It is up to you to consider what you will gain from going to court and letting a judge decide your outcome.

You need to be realistic in any of these resolution models.

>What is the best possible outcome for you?

>And from the opposite perspective,

>What is the worst possible outcome for you?

## Litigation is public!

It is a simple process for any interested party to go on-line and find a lot of the various documents that make up a lawsuit, yours included. This allows investors and potential buyers of a company as a part of their due diligence, to read court pleadings and get a feel for your corporate culture. Similarly, and perhaps more importantly to you as a team leader, potential employees can read court filings as a part of their reference checking when they are considering joining your company.

## The dollars!

Put simply, it will cost you more money the longer your dispute continues, and the more litigious it becomes.

Even if you have a bottomless bucket of cash, and you're happy for the lawyers to wallow in it, there are many other considerations to weigh up before wasting your time and energy in lawyers chambers and courtrooms, as we have already discussed.

It is also worth noting that while the Dispute Resolution Continuum chart can overlay the Conflict Continuum chart, this isn't always the case. Often conflicts can be resolved by negotiation or mediation, and sometimes complaints go straight to litigation.

## 'Avoidance' or sticking your head in the sand

A wise man once wrote, "There is no avoidance in delay". It was actually a fellow called Aeschylus and the quote is from his ancient Greek play, Agamemnon.

Maybe I shouldn't be calling it avoidance at all, because if you are avoiding a messy situation, you are really only putting it off to deal with down the track. If this is your management style then it is going to create more (difficult) work later on. You might as well start dealing with it now, and save yourself some pain in the long run.

While you don't want to micro-manage every situation in your team, it is important to know what issues people are concerned with, and where any heightened conflict is appearing. This is where we reflect on why you should be having your stand-up coffee meetings regularly. In those coffee meetings you can monitor the interaction and communication of the team in a relaxed setting. By holding (and attending) these short informal meetings regularly, you will see who's talking to who (or not).  Because you have been holding these informal meetings regularly, you will know your staff better, and you will probably notice any relationship changes more easily.  Now you will be able to talk to those involved more casually about issues concerning them, before they escalate.

## Back to Avoidance

By not being aware of staff relationship changes, or noticing that a particular topic has become a hot button around the team, you are encouraging a breeding ground for conflict to develop and progress up to the next level.

You need to stay aware of your team, stay connected to them and their concerns, and they will respect you for it.  To have staff come to you with their conflicts or for advice is great, but don't expect them to.  It takes time to develop that level of respect and trust from team members.

Also remember that you are dealing with a wide range of personalities in any team who all need managing in different ways.  Both the extrovert and the introvert could have the same concept, but they would present it in a very different format.  The extrovert may come in full of bravado and self-confidence, while the introvert may present in a much more humble style. Both presentation styles may have great merit, but be conscious not to let yourself get fixated on one or the other. Your role as the leader is to get the best out of all your staff, while ensuring they feel they are contributing in a useful way. Blending the human resources you have into an effective functioning team will go a long way to increasing the overall productivity of the team.

Dealing with conflict as it arises will be a day to day activity. We do not live in a conflict free world or workplace. A workplace without minor conflict would be like a world where everybody looked and acted the same, very boring.

## The creative conflict in Monty Python's Flying Circus

To have conflict is to be stimulated, to have others challenge the way you do things provokes your own thinking. When confronted or challenged by others you need to justify your ideas and explain the why's and how's of your concept. Without conflict we would be not be inspired, that irritating conflict can be the spark that's needed to ignite the flame for the next big idea.

John Cleese writes in his latest book (So, Anyway...) about the writing style for Monty Python's Flying Circus. Cleese explains that he and Graham Chapman would write as a team, and the others in the Circus would pair up to work on their ideas similarly. At the end of each week the whole group would gather and knock the sketches about until they were satisfied with them. The book describes some very intense discussions about the writing, especially between Cleese and Terry Jones. At the end of these sessions though, they had amazing content to record, which has gone on to become some of the most iconic comedy the world has ever seen.

Without that intense conflict and challenging of ideas, Monty Pythons Flying Circus may have been just another sketch comedy show that was lost to the seventies. The fact that the Flying Circus were able to reform a few years ago and fill the O2 stadium in London several times, is a testament to how good the material was that came out of that conflict and passion.

Cleese explains in his book that the dominant emotion was exasperation rather than anger, and that Cleese and Jones acted as useful counterweights to each other. The conflict enabled each member of the group to express and demonstrate their concerns, which resulted in some of the most influential comedy the world has ever seen.

If managed correctly the same can work for your team, a little bit of conflict can be very constructive to spark expression of ideas.

## Know when to step in

The difficult part is to recognise when conflict goes from being healthy and creative, to being detrimental and harmful to the group.  This is the challenge for every manager and team leader.  How far can you let the disagreement build before stepping in?  If you step in too early you risk the possibility of missing out on that next big idea, and quashing the creative spirit.  If you leave it too late, you may be inviting bullying and harassment claims, or even litigation.  So what to do?

This is the question, and it's where you need to know your people and your team.  How much is too much for them, where is the line in the sand, and of course because its sand, it's always moving.  The better you know your staff, and the more open and comfortable your working relationship is with them, the easier it will be to know where that line in the sand is, if it is overstepped, and how and why to resolve those differences early.

And we are back to productivity again.  While it might be very nice to be working in a happy respectful environment, with everyone smiling and cheerful all the time, that's not how life or work is.  Activities can go off the rails and people will argue, but it's not unmanageable.

What is unmanageable is letting these arguments get out of control, or avoiding them until they are highly developed.

That's when productivity suffers, and when it takes a lot of time and energy to get those activities and people back into a manageable situation. If you can put the effort into effectively managing people when the disputes are small, you can respectfully control these situations. This is where the time and energy savings are, and is where productivity can really grow.

# Chapter 11

# The Monetary Cost of Conflict and the Conflict Calculator

I have discussed a lot about hidden costs and intangibles that are difficult to measure in monetary terms. Losses and increases in productivity are problematic to measure at the best of times. Productivity can be complex to determine on a long term or even a quarterly basis, so how do we measure change in the short term?

Most productivity indexes take a divisional or whole of company view, while what I am discussing with you in this book is on a more personal level, making the changes much more subtle. You may notice changes in communication styles between staff, or the way your team meetings run. You might also notice staff come to you more often with challenges (and hopefully options for solutions).

The change you are looking for in your team is in its culture. Are you building a team culture by default or by design? As the leader, be the example others want to follow. If you want to see excellence, be excellent first.

If you want more from people create a fire within them, not under them, and thank them often. People forget praise quickly, but remember reprimands for a long time, so be thankful often.

## Extra reading

If you are interested in learning more about how to measure productivity, then I have an excellent article for you to read. This article was published in the Harvard Business Review in 1988, but is still relevant and worth reading. https://hbr.org/1988/01/no-nonsense-guide-to-measuring-productivity

W. Bruce Chew discusses that there are many ways to measure productivity, but unless the system and index is simple, there isn't a lot of value in it. He also found that many companies spend more money on measuring productivity than they could possibly save in their findings.

My number one takeaway from Chew's article is that there is more to productivity than the cost of making a product. How do you include the value of the engineering team that develops an improvement that will affect a production line for years into the future? Increasing productivity starts with you, the team leader.

## The conflict cost calculator

The conflict cost calculator which is available to download from my website (www.mimmediation.net), is designed to attach monetary values to what we have been talking about in the previous chapters. While the calculator will never give you an exact dollar amount because of the number of variables, it will give you valuable data to evaluate. It will also give you a sense of the costs involved, and a better understanding of the drain that conflict has in monetary terms.

## Overview of the calculator

The calculator firstly asks direct questions about the amount of time and wages of those involved directly and indirectly in the conflict. What is the average number of hours that each person involved has spent away from their normal work activities? This is where you include all the time these people have actually spent disagreeing or being distracted from their usual work, because they are talking about the conflict with others.

As I mentioned, this is not an exact science and even this first task is subjective. However by putting numbers to these questions, you are constructing the foundations on which to build on.

By including as much information as you can on this and subsequent conflicts, clear patterns will emerge on which you can act.

## Cost of HR and management

This task is similar to the first, but involves the amount of time your human resources department spent on this particular conflict. Here you are asked specifics of how much time has been spent on intervening, strategising, supervising and documenting the dispute.

While HR is always going to have this type of work to do, if this particular conflict didn't need them to be involved, what else could they be doing? This question considers the productivity costs to the HR department; overheads that every company has, but that can be minimised through effective team management and early dispute resolution.

The calculator also asks about sick days and unscheduled personal leave days that were taken as a result of the conflict. Conflicts and disagreements can take an unexpected toll on many people. Sometimes current events and having to deal with other people's conflict will trigger experiences from their own past that amplify emotions in them. In some instances, people will need time off to recover from being exposed to these situations and conversations.

## Vicarious Trauma

The effect of hearing about and dealing with traumatic events of others, also known as vicarious trauma, is more often referred to in counselling professions. I first learned about vicarious trauma through my Lifeline experience working on their crisis phone line, where we were given excellent training and support in this area. While not widely discussed in the human resource industry, HR professionals are subject to vicarious trauma and need support too.

The accumulative build-up from listening and helping others deal with their difficult situations can develop into seriously stressful situations, which need to be monitored by managers. The advice I've had from Lifeline and others on this subject is to ensure people talk through anything that might concern them, or plays on their mind. No-one can conduct their job at their best if they are stressed over other people's problems.

Talking helps, so start talking, discussing your concerns if you or anyone else you think of needs help in this area. Many companies have confidential counselling programs that are easy to access through HR departments or managers. If you have no-one else to talk to, then a GP or crisis phone line is a great place to start as they can assist with referrals to many services.

## Measuring the cost, one conflict at a time

It's important to note here that this calculator is to evaluate one conflict at a time. Its purpose is to drill down into one particular disagreement and analyse the monetary cost of that issue to the company. Completed to the best of your ability and regularly, you will begin to understand where the hidden costs are, and develop a plan to do something about it. The more data you accumulate, the better the resource you are creating for future use.

## Employee turnover

We have discussed employee turnover in some detail earlier in this book, so I'm not going to go over it all again here. In connection to the calculator though, there are a few questions relating to employee turnover.

How many staff have left the company, what was their salary and if any, what severance was paid?

The remaining implications discussed earlier on staff turnover is even more difficult to measure, considering how subjective it all is. To counter some of this inaccuracy, the calculator offers a factoring option. There is a factor set for any professional or managerial staff turnover, which you can alter as you see fit. This factoring allows for variables such as:

1. How long is it going to take until the vacant position is filled?

2. What will you spend on advertising and resumé screening?

3. How long will the interview process take?

4. The cost of other staff filling the vacant role

5. Behavioural screenings, skills assessments and background checking costs

6. Any transport and travel related expenses

Hopefully by now you are seeing the value in this exercise, even though it is difficult to capture all of the costs, or know how accurate they are. Although this is a rough guide, please remember that by completing the exercise, you will gain valuable data and insight.

The data gathered from this single incident is valuable in seeing what one conflict has cost the company, and by conducting this exercise over several or all of your conflicts, you can use this data in a variety of situations.

1. You may use it as a tool when presenting to HR, requesting additional staff to reduce stress related turnover

2. Senior management will be interested in the data as evidence of hidden costs and patterns of conflict

3. For your own benefit, you will see patterns within your team, department and staff

Once you have sufficient data from performing a number of calculations, you can go back and conduct a mind mapping exercise dedicated to one particular area of concern that you have identified. And so it becomes a continual process of improvement for you and your team.

## Lost Income

This one is pretty straight forward. How many billable hours did the company lose, and what was the average dollar value of every lost hour? You may be able to access this information from HR or your accounts department, depending on your particular company. The more accurate the information the better, but whatever you provide is better than nothing.

## Increased Expenses

This section discusses litigation and workers compensation claims. What, if any costs were incurred for this dispute in regard to lawyers, solicitors, mediators, fines, claims or any other billed costs?

Again, any figures you can provide will be of benefit. Different companies will have different policies about divulging this type of information, so anything you can obtain is better than nothing.

## Restructuring costs

Another subjective question, but this is the last question and it's about any restructuring costs. Think about time spent on changes to job descriptions, reassigning work tasks, or redesigning reporting relationships with those involved. Take some time to consider other structural changes made as a result of the conflict. Was there a special taskforce or committee assigned to work on improvements because of this particular conflict? Research suggests the costs of such changes are around 10% of combined wages of those involved.

## Finished – Well done

Congratulations on finishing your first conflict calculation. As you do more of these calculations you will become quicker and more critical in the estimation of the actual costs for each question. Like anything, the more you complete, the more proficient you will become.

This really is a significant tool for you in grasping the value in resolving disputes early. Over time, the data gathered from numerous conflicts will serve you well to comprehend the costs involved in all sorts of disagreements. From the small, quickly settled conflict, to long running unresolved disputes, the calculator will show you how important it is to resolve them as early as possible.

Keep up the good work in analysing the data you gather, work on improvements with others, and enhanced results will follow.

## Dr Tammy Lenski

The calculator is a great tool and I must thank Dr Tammy Lenski for allowing me to use it here. I have modified it slightly from Tammy's original, but the concept is hers and you can find out more about Tammy from this link: http://lenski.com

Tammy is a respected author and mediator, and founded her conflict resolution firm in 1997. Please take some time to look at her work as she is a leader in mediation and conflict resolution.

## Conflict Matrix

I also use a conflict matrix alongside the conflict calculator, which you can download from my website, www.mimmediation.net .  Again, this is another simple tool which helps to visualise and document where your conflicts are appearing.

The matrix simply lists the various types of conflict possible down one side, and the level of the conflict across the top.  For instance, was it a financial, process, or communication issue, and how did you rate it on the conflict continuum?

The matrix is initially for each individual conflict, and would be attached to its file.  From there you can input this information into a spread sheet to build up a database over time, where you can see any hot spots or trends developing.

## Confidentiality and privacy

It is important to remember that most of the information you are dealing with during these conflicts is confidential, so you should check your company policy and procedures to ensure you are compliant in this area.  Remember, people's names and private information requires special consideration at all times.  Where and how this personal information is to be recorded for your company will be in those policy and procedure documents. Please check them before proceeding.

## 'Double the benefit' increases productivity

The cost calculator is excellent in analysing past conflicts and seeing how much these disagreements have cost in the past. Aside from that however, it becomes a wonderful incentive to repair new conflicts early. Once you are aware how much conflicts have cost your department, you should be more enthusiastic to resolve them earlier.

I'm reflecting now on the recurring issues we discussed in chapter nine. As highlighted in that chapter, once you are aware of an issue, you can work towards eliminating it. Once you eliminate (or at least reduce) the occurrence, the savings in time and money may be complicated to see, but they definitely exist.

The act of removing every single conflict actually doubles the productivity gain. The financial and time savings related to resolving any issue allows you to spend that time and money on more beneficial activities for your company, successfully increasing productivity.

Done well, that issue may never reappear, and as a consequence, you have also produced the 'hidden passive income' discussed earlier.

# Chapter 12

# What's Your Dispute Resolution Plan and Where Does Mediation fit?

## Back to me for a minute

You may have noticed by now that I am a mediator. I have been able to defuse conflict in many situations as a part of my natural DNA. I've been able to talk my way in and out of a few interesting situations in the past, and I've also helped others work through difficult times. Over the past few years I have transformed this communication skill into my career, through my work on the crisis phone lines at Lifeline, and subsequently by becoming a nationally qualified mediator in Australia.

I have a genuine passion for this work; helping others move on with their lives and get past issues and conflict that have been consuming them for too long. The work can be very rewarding, while at other times very frustrating and exhausting. It is however always a privilege to be allowed into someone's confidence, and be given the opportunity to help them through a difficult time.

## What do you know?

As Donald Rumsfeld, United States Secretary of Defence (1975-77 & 2001-06) simply put it,

There are known knowns. These are things we know that we know.

There are known unknowns. That is to say, there are things that we know we don't know.

But there are also unknown unknowns. There are things we don't know we don't know.

Rumsfeld's quote makes me stop and consider what we think we know and how easy it is to go into situations with unconscious assumptions.

Firstly, the known knowns. As a mediator I understand the processes, mechanics and obligations that make mediation the conflict resolution the success it is. Of course confidentiality is extremely important throughout mediation, from the very first meeting or intake interview, right through to the signed agreements at the end of the process. Parties can move on with their lives knowing that the whole episode is behind them and finished with. Participants need to be confident that their privacy is respected and contained throughout the entire mediation process.

Setting boundaries, guidelines and rules from the outset, then getting people to agree to, abide by, and sign those rules is also very important. This is primarily done so that people understand what those boundaries and guidelines are, but also to enable the mediator to bring the mediation back within those rules if anyone oversteps them.

Secondly, what do I not know? I don't know a lot of things, and when going into a mediation, that is important. While I understand in detail how the mediation process works, I don't need (or want) to know too much about the situation I'm getting involved in prior to meeting the people who are actually living the conflict. When I talk to the people in the conflict for the first time, I want to hear their experience of it without any influence or prejudice from what others have told me. I'll talk more about these 'intake interviews' later in this chapter.

Lastly, Rumsfeld's quote makes me think about how issues might have changed since I last considered them. I don't know what I don't know. I am always learning from my own personal experiences, while also reading and learning from other people. Change is happening around us all of the time; we are constantly adapting and modifying what we know and believe to be true because of these changes. What I have judged as true in the past may not be true anymore, because of other people's changes.

## Case Study

On returning from a 12 month secondment, one manager knew of the broad outline of changes in her team because she had had informal conversations with some of her team during her time away. However she was unaware of the more subtle details of the changes, and needed to spend time learning the impacts of these changes on the whole team. The changes while this manager had been absent had impacted her senior managers, and also those reporting into the team. She needed to be fully briefed to understand the implications of the changes, before instilling further changes on the team. Without taking the time to understand the impact and detail of the changes in this example, it would have been easy for the manager to assume how these changes had affected the team, and to have made poor decisions on her return.

I hope some of what you have read in these chapters has challenged you and made you look at conflict differently.

>Ensure you know what you should know.

## Current policy and procedures

Whether or not you know the details and procedures of your conflict resolution policy, now is a great time to ensure your knowledge is up to date in this area. Hopefully you know where to find these documents, and can access them easily. Take the time now to review or summarise your policy and procedures so you are familiar with them before proceeding.

The structure of your policy regarding your conflict resolution plan will determine the effectiveness of it, how complaints escalate, and how long disputes take to resolve.

Sometimes the delay in dealing with complaints is caused by confusing, contradictory or inappropriate complaint handling policy and procedures. These documents do not always reflect current thinking or awareness, and good policy and procedures will have a review date. Check this date and advise whoever is responsible if a review is overdue.

Your conflict resolution plan should be able to handle the full range of disputes, including:

a.      Internal disputes between all levels of staff and employees in the workplace.

b.      Customer and consumer disputes about your products and services.

c.      External business related disputes - suppliers, contractors and other service providers.

d.      Wider community disputes, including government agencies, local councils, neighbours and other stakeholders

## What is a typical dispute resolution process?

Most companies have a dispute resolution policy that covers the basics of dealing with conflict at work, and certainly larger companies are well equipped with the tools and processes to facilitate conflict resolution.

Five main dispute resolution processes exist for workplace and business disputes. Generally, as the dispute escalates, the cost in terms of time, money and effort increase, while privacy decreases. I've outlined them briefly here first, and will go into further detail below.

1.	A negotiated outcome where the parties involved resolve the dispute themselves.

2.	A facilitated outcome where an internal facilitator helps the parties to reach a resolution between them.

3.	A mediated outcome where an independent mediator helps the parties resolve the dispute between them.

4.	An arbitrated outcome where an independent arbitrator determines how the dispute is to be resolved.

5.	A court process where a judge or jury determines how the dispute is to be resolved, and makes a binding court order.


Take a look at the steps in detail now and evaluate how your company's policy compares.

# 1. A negotiated outcome where the parties involved resolve the dispute themselves

**Talk to each other**

I know this can be part of the problem, so excuse me for stating the obvious, but sometimes it's worth reminding people. If the only communication has been through emails or another platform, having a face to face conversation can sometimes 'clear the air'. This is the first step to reconciliation and may or may not work for you.

If feel uncomfortable talking to the other party alone, then include someone else in the first instance. It's always better to have someone else with you for support and as a witness, rather than facing the other party alone. As a general rule, your manager will want to know what you have done to attempt to work things out before taking the matter any further.

2. **A facilitated outcome where an internal facilitator helps the parties to reach a resolution between them**

   a. **Engagement with the direct manager.**

      If this manager is you, then this is the opportunity to use your knowledge and current relationship to resolve the situation. This is what I have been discussing throughout the book, and where as the manager, you can have a real impact on the individuals involved by settling the matter in the early stages of the dispute. Coming up with a realistic solution that will work for everyone now stops all the conflict that can follow.

      All the costs in time and money, as well as the mental anguish that can affect those involved, can be stopped at this stage.
      This is where knowing your staff and understanding their motivations pays off, all those stand-up meetings where you have been listening and chatting with them, interacting and gaining their trust. When your staff trust and respect you, you have already created the environment to work with them to resolve the issue.

b.  **Senior management get involved.**

>Your direct manager might talk to their manager next. This can be another attempt to settle the affair informally. Please remember the Dispute Resolution Continuum in chapter 10, where we discussed how much simpler it is to resolve a conflict on the informal side of the chart, before the issue moves too far across to the right and becomes more complicated.

c.  **HR become involved.**

>Now the conflict is starting to involve more people, time, and other resources, and is getting more serious for everyone. HR will probably hold meetings in an attempt to settle the disagreement in-house. While this can work, and HR departments resolve many conflicts, sometimes the parties involved feel that HR isn't impartial. People can feel that HR is biased, as they might have had previous experience with a particular HR individual which has made them feel they won't get a fair hearing.

>It could be that the HR department is looked on as being on the side of the company and not neutral,

that they will simply do 'what's best for the company'.  Even if this is not true, once someone has that concept in their mind, it can be almost impossible to change.  HR is an important and essential part of every company, but they are not the best or only mechanism to deal with every conflict.

A good HR team and policy will know when and how to engage outside assistance.

# 3. A mediated outcome where an independent mediator helps the parties to resolve the dispute between them.

Mediations are usually face to face, with all parties in the same room (so long as it is safe), although recent advances are seeing more on-line mediations conducted.  As a part of the process, intake interviews are held with each party separately before the actual mediation to help them prepare.

Mediation is an informal process that generally doesn't require legal representation, although employees and employers are able to bring support people by agreement. Even when support people and/or lawyers are present, the mediator will only communicate directly with the people affected by the dispute. Private sessions may be held during a mediation to discuss issues that arise, and can be called for by any party.

You should always look for a mediator who is Nationally Accredited, impartial, and agrees to uphold the highest ethical standards. All parties must be comfortable with, and accepting of the chosen mediator.

Engaging an external independent mediator is a step that is sometimes overlooked, and many companies head straight for a government agency (e.g. Fair Work Australia), when their internal processes don't reach a satisfactory conclusion. For those who already feel daunted by the progression of events they have endured, that step, of facing a government agency, is a huge leap for many individuals, and can put them at a significant disadvantage.

Using a government organisation is a viable option, but they can have longer waiting periods than an independent mediator who can often start proceedings within a matter of days.

Always remember that in mediation, you have the ability to stop proceedings at any time or walk away. You are in control throughout the mediation and you can ask questions, request a private session, or a break when you need it. Often a short break or a private session with the mediator will provide insight or an unrealised perspective. Bringing those new perspectives back to the mediation table can unlock a stalemate, and encourage discussions towards an alternative solution.

Mediation can be your best option, but it does require preparation, effort and flexibility from everyone.

## 4. An arbitrated outcome where an independent arbitrator determines how the dispute is to be resolved.

Looking back at the Dispute Resolution Continuum in chapter 10 again, arbitrated outcomes are now in the hands of the arbitrator, and as such, the parties have lost some control. Issues are also likely to be getting more costly, more public, and probably more stressful.

The time and energy that it takes to get this far can be extreme for some, and the mental anguish can take its toll. Care needs to be taken with everyone's emotional state at all times, and re-evaluated regularly.

While much of the process during arbitration is similar to mediation, and you are not yet in court, it is another step towards litigation and as such, is painful in many ways.

If you are in this situation you should consider all costs, including your mental and physical health.

Before you get any more heavily involved in any of these processes (mediation, arbitration or a court process), you need to consider if what you are asking for is worth the anguish you may have to go through? Be realistic and evaluate (with others), what would be the best possible outcome for you, and also what is the worst possible outcome for you. Take the time for a regular reality check to evaluate your situation, and ensure you understand all possible outcomes before proceeding.

You are now getting involved in a serious chain of events, and you must look after yourself and others that you are responsible for. What are the implications for you, and your staff's families especially?

## 5. A court process where a judge or jury determines how the dispute is to be resolved and makes a binding court order.

I would think that most people have a reasonable understanding of the process and principals involved in going to court, and I have highlighted the pros and cons of getting to this point several times already in this book. It's enough to say that you need to be quite robust and appreciate the consequences of the judge's decision.

By this stage you have handed over a large portion of control to your legal team to state your case, and the judge will hand down their decision as they see fit.

As stated previously, you must understand and be aware of all possible outcomes before going to court; otherwise you may be severely disheartened and frustrated in the judge's ruling at the end of it all.

## Mediation Intake interviews

Having briefly discussed intake interviews earlier, I'll go into more detail now.

Each party meets the mediator separately from all other parties. They are encouraged to have a support person or people with them at these meetings. Intake interviews can be in the days or weeks before mediation, or on the same day. They can be conducted over the phone, in person, or on-line.

These intake interviews are for the mediator to:

1.      Listen and gain an understanding of what has brought each party to the mediation. It also allows the parties to ask the mediator questions.

2.      Hear the detail of what has happened to each person directly involved.

3.      Explain and prepare the parties for what actually happens in mediation - what are the steps on the day.

4.      Get informed consent from the parties.

5. Discuss the cost of not resolving the issue.

6. Ensure mediation is appropriate for each party and that they have the capacity to participate. In this phase the mediator will check for:

   a. Violence – is it safe for everyone to be in the same room? Consider conducting the mediation on-line or over the phone as alternatives.

   b. Mental health issues – does the mediation have the potential to cause harm to anyone's mental health?

   c. Motivation – what is the actual motivation, and are there any hidden agendas?

   d. Substance abuse – is anyone involved affected, or likely to be affected by drugs or alcohol?

   e. Power balance – is there an unfair advantage to one side. e.g. CEO vs production line employee.

If any of the above is apparent, mediation needs to be reconsidered. There is little point in pursuing mediation if one or more of these factors are at work.

## Do you feel comfortable with your current conflict resolution policy and procedure?

I hope you do, and if not, that I have provided you with enough tools and information to realise some of your unknown unknowns.

The ball is now back in your court. You now have the knowledge to question and challenge why your policy is the way it is. Does it need improving, and would it improve with the addition of extra elements? Depending on your company will be where you go from here. HR is often the holders of policy improvement, although larger companies may have a compliance department who is responsible for managing policy and procedure.

If you have any questions that you would like me to answer directly, please drop me a line at malguy@mimmediation.net or visit www.mimmediation.net to stay in touch.

# Chapter 13

# Stopping the Head hunters -

# Or at Least Slowing Them Down

What if you could stop staff from moving on whenever they were approached by a head hunter? How would that improve your productivity?

In today's world staff transition from job to job much more frequently than in the past. Long gone are the days when you got a job and stayed for life.

> 'Ninety-one percent of Millennials (born between 1977-1997) expect to stay in a job for less than three years, according to the Future Workplace "Multiple Generations @ Work" survey of 1,189 employees and 150 managers. That means they would have 15 – 20 jobs over the course of their working lives!'

The point is, the longer you retain your staff, the less you burden HR, the longer you preserve (and increase) CIP – Corporate Intellectual Property, and the more likely you are of developing a positive team culture.

## The room of mirrors

This chapter revolves around how you treat yourself and your staff, and whether or not they want to work in your team. The fact that a large percentage of people leave their job because they can't, or don't want to work with their boss is something you can change.

You might need to find a room of mirrors and have a good hard look at yourself, but if you have reached this far in this book, you are probably doing some of that already. You might be questioning why you do certain things, and be considering management style changes even now.

## Why and when staff chooses to leave your team starts the day they start.

We often assume that we are the centre of the universe, that our world is the most important, and that ours is the only view that matters.

Sadly for us this isn't true. New staff had a life before we meet them, and will continue their lives well after they leave our company or team. What's important here is that we connect with new staff in a way that somehow enhances their motivation.

## So what does motivate people?

Motivation arises from what's important to the individual, so the skill for the manager is to discover what that motivation is.

Motivation can come from almost anywhere, and it depends on people's individual goals.

a. Money of course is a very strong motivator. Once the money is there, different choices and motivations open up.

b. Career ambitions - is this job a stepping stone in a bigger plan?

c. Family and work/life balance. People have different needs depending on their family situation. Staff with young children will have different motivations to empty nesters and singles.

d.  Friends and hobbies are often motivators.  It might be essential for a local sports coach to be able leave work early to get to the club to attend training for instance.

Remember, motivations can change as well, the single driven colleague who has always worked extended hours can change dramatically, simply because they fall in love.

## No Hidden Agenda!

From the very first day somebody new comes into your team, you can ask them what they expect from you and their new role.  You can ask them directly or indirectly, what do you want out of this role and how can I help you achieve that.

Indirect questioning will allow people to freely divulge information that you won't get by asking directly.  For instance, you wouldn't/can't ask someone when they are thinking of having their next child, but you can ask what you would like to be doing in two years' time.  I know senior managers who use this style of indirect questioning once they have built rapport in interviews or performance reviews, and people do open up to them.

The point is that by engaging with people at the beginning of their working relationship with an open agenda, you can discover their motivations, and work on a path to reach both of your goals together. To have an open working relationship from the outset with new team members lets them know where they stand with you, and hopefully where you stand with them.

As a disclaimer, I must admit that this won't work every time, and some people won't open up to you as much as others. The objective here is not to win everyone over, but to set the landscape for the relationship so that expectations are laid out as early as possible without hidden agendas.

## How does a new employee know your team culture?

This open style of communication does take more time than you may be used to spending with your staff, but time spent here can eliminate hours in conflict later. When you construct this understanding of open communication from the outset, you set up the ability to discuss absolutely anything throughout your working relationship with these people.

New staff learns team culture by example, not from a company manual or slogan. Employees will learn your team culture early and quickly, so make it a point to connect with your new staff at the earliest possible time. Leaving this task to someone else is like letting someone else raise your children, you won't know what they are teaching them!

## Forewarned is forearmed

Utilising this style you can discuss career paths and development without the fear of surprise. If you know a person's career goals early in the relationship, then together you can plan career development, succession planning and projects that compliment and develop that particular person. Discussing the plan along the way is important too, motivations change as do timelines, but so long as you are aware of these changes, you can modify the plan.

Example:

## Maternity leave

This is probably the most common long term staff planning companies complete at present, and is a great example of how this can work in other areas. With maternity leave, managers and HR are often advised 6 months in advance.

Managers are notified of:

a. the date the baby is due

b. when the staff member plans to stop work

c. the various doctors' appointments along the way; and

d. how long the mum plans to be away after the birth

This is standard practice for HR and managers in all maternity leave planning, and yet it is seldom applied in any other part of the workplace.

Maternity leave planning allows for continuity of work as one person phases out of the team, and her responsibilities are allocated to others while she is away. Secondments are often part of the plan, or temp staff are bought in to fill the gap.

## Transferring the example

My point with the example above is that this approach to staff movements can be applied to most positions in a team. When you know someone is planning to leave months in advance, you are able to plan and transition with much more certainty. And yes, I know people will say this type of planning happens already, but I believe it can be encouraged and developed much more than it currently is.

If managers are aware of why staff are thinking of leaving, perhaps they can amend the role to retain them longer, or at least talk about it. If people are leaving because they aren't being challenged in their current role, again changes can be made.

My objective with this topic is to broaden your discussions with your staff to open up possibilities of training and engagement. If people are reluctant to discuss such topics, then do you really want them working with you? How long are they going to stay anyway?

# Lifeline suicide questioning

In my early training at Lifeline I was taught to ask callers directly, "are you thinking about suicide or taking your own life?" It's never the first question I ask, but as soon as I believe they may be at risk, I will find a way to ask them this question directly. I was taught to question callers in this way to be certain that there is no misunderstanding about what we are talking about. In any conversation that might be about suicide, if the caller is thinking about taking their own life, I need to know as soon as possible. If they aren't suicidal, they will say so and we can talk about something else, but if they are, then they need to be asked directly.

This direct style of questioning can be transferred straight into conversations with staff when you think they might be looking for another job. Why not simply ask them "are you looking for another job?" You might find a slightly different way of asking such a question, but it needs to be unmistakable that you are asking about their career movement.

Of course not everyone will answer truthfully, but for those who do, you have an incredible opportunity to discuss why, and how they have got to the point of wanting to leave their current role. Just like asking 'the suicide question', by talking about why someone is thinking about changing jobs, you are able to talk about why they might like to stay. Any ambivalence of 'should I stay or should I go' can then be worked through together, and a path forward can be forged with both parties knowing where they are headed.

## Ask very direct questions to find underlying issues

When we ask direct questions about suicide or changing jobs, this can open up a whole new dialogue about underlying issues that we didn't even realise were there. Talking helps, but unless you take the time to ask and then listen, you cannot learn. The reason the person wants to leave might be something you can fix, and if you know this early enough and want them to stay, you may be able to find a solution.

Once you are aware of a staff member who wants to leave, you can offer options that might make them stay, or make plans to transfer information to others before they leave. The cost of someone leaving your team without giving adequate notice can be damaging. The loss of CIP that is taken with them without the sufficient transfer of information can slow projects and reduce productivity incredibly.

## Maintaining the standard

This early establishment of open communication and the ability to discuss important personal issues needs to be continued throughout the entire time staff is with you. This is an ongoing standard and culture you are upholding, and over time it will become your natural style, but it also needs monitoring on your part and be something you can work into your superior's review of you too.

Performance reviews are the obvious professional opportunities to talk about goals, motivations and expectations with your staff, but these types of discussions can be held at other times as well. The need to keep communication lines open and inviting is paramount, and you should always be ready for invitations to evaluate these higher level themes.

## Creating walking billboards

Another of the interesting aspects about creating open communication environments is that when employees do leave, you can still maintain a healthy relationship with them. As they transition out of your workforce, they can become an external asset to you and your company. What better advertisement could you have than to be able to refer a new employee or prospect to this positive walking, talking commercial? To have ex-staff talking positively about you and your company out in the community is to have a walking billboard, and that in itself is a rare commodity in a lot of industries.

The alternative is a disgruntled ex-employee who is ready and willing at any moment to fire off insults and negative comments whenever they are asked about your company or you.

Which walking billboard would you rather have out there expressing experiences of their time spent with you?

## Reality check

You will never stop people from moving on no matter how hard you work at it, and neither should you if their needs or motivation are elsewhere. You can however slow down the coming and going of staff in your team.

The revolving door of employees has significant effects on your productivity when you are constantly training new staff, and re-establishing the CIP accounts as they learn the ropes of your team and company. When you slow down that revolving door and increase the average time staff stay within your team, you create extra time for yourself to work on the more productive parts of your role and self-development.

# Chapter 14

"Leadership is a verb not a noun. Leaders act; and their actions either speak for or against them."

General Sir Peter Cosgrove

Australian Governor General 2014-

# Conclusion - Gardening

## Thanks

Well done and thanks for making it to the last chapter of my book. I want to recap here and draw parallels between developing a productive team, and a gardener who is striving to produce an exceptional plot.

My apologies for all the bad puns throughout this chapter, but hopefully this helps you to remember the themes I have been cultivating.

## The productivity gardener

This whole higher productivity objective which we work towards is one which we take on with little training. To get the best out of people and assets, we for the most, learn on the job as we go and do the best we can. So by transplanting productivity into the concept of tending a garden, we can examine how your day to day tasks produce your culture and showpiece for the world to see. In the process, as in a healthy garden, productivity will flourish.

## Taking over a new garden

When you move into a new home you often inherit a garden as well. Similarly, when you move into a new role at work, you inherit staff, furnishings, a culture, and the productivity that comes along with it. What you do with what have 'come in to' is up to you.

You can leave it alone and see what happens. This is unlikely to produce any improvement, although there might be a lovely section in one corner that will keep on producing great results without any immediate input from you. On the other hand, you may have a section that is overgrown from neglect, and will need a whole lot of work to get anything productive out of it at all.

## Understanding foundations and positioning

Taking on a new team is a great responsibility, and getting it right at the start is imperative.  My preferred method of exploring the foundations and positioning of any new environment is to mind map as early as I can - to understand how the land lies.  Mind mapping in this instance might involve a few or all of the team members to get an overview of tasks, projects, priorities, staff and issues.  As we know from earlier chapters, mind mapping can be completed quickly to gain insight into any complex situation, which is exactly what you need at the beginning of any new role.

From this first mind mapping session you can start to plan how you want to improve sections, or reposition structural components of the team.  I'm not suggesting you drive a bulldozer through the place and completely demolish everything in your first month; that is not the way to develop trust and respect in a new team.

You still need to be able to function and produce the goods, so this is more of a gradual renovation rather than a complete rip out and rebuild.  Some aspects of a garden take a long time to develop, while other smaller parts might be an instant replace. You can be looking at long term big picture improvement, while also concentrating on the smaller day to day incremental changes.

## Landscaping and time-lining

Once you understand the current structure and foundations of your patch you can begin to timeline the improvements. Are there hedges you can't see over, thorny, overgrown patches that need clearing, or sections that just need a little bit of maintenance in the short term, and can wait for further development later?

I would naturally start with the simpler tasks, while preparing the groundwork for larger projects. Tackling a few small jobs early will show others that you are working on improvements, and start building respect and trust in those around you.

## Clearing thorny patches

There may be large thorny patches that have become overgrown through neglect or left to their own natural untidy growth. These are the underperforming territories that have become an eyesore to everyone and need to be confronted sooner rather than later.

More time is required planning, mind mapping again, and building resources before venturing into these areas. When tackling these zones you need to be prepared. You cannot afford to transform these areas without the right tools and the right people to assist you. These areas are visible to everyone, and many will know they need fixing, so plenty of people will be watching with interest to see what you do to these areas.

As you begin to transform these underperforming areas you will come under scrutiny from other managers, staff and departments. Be as open as you can in these projects, without compromising confidentiality. As always, confidentiality is paramount when dealing with people, and you must be mindful of this at all times.

## Replanting with the right stuff

Just like in a garden, within your team you have the opportunity to remove dead wood and open up space for replanting or new growth. Caution here is of the utmost importance; removing dead wood at the workplace requires a much more delicate touch than in a garden, no heavy machinery is recommended.

At other times, natural cycles and attrition will allow you the opportunity to bring in fresh faces.

When you do have the occasion to replant, ensure that you select the best specimens you are able to find.  The right selection here will enhance productivity, and with careful integration as discussed in chapter 13, you can cultivate long and fruitful relationships.

## Weeding, Composting, Recycling and Feedback

I consider weeding in conflict management as being on the lookout for little disagreements, knowing that you don't need to pull out every tiny weed in your garden, but be aware of what people are concerned about.  Keep an eye on the issues, and when you notice them getting to a size that requires your intervention, go in and resolve the dispute before it gets too large.

As you prune and clip the excess in your garden to make your compost, so too can you gather data and experience from your team members and feed that back to them in a similar way.  I'm told that "Feedback is the breakfast of champions" (Clinton Swaine, www.frontiertrainings.com), and as compost is the feedback for gardens, whichever way you look at this, feedback is critical to growth and an important part of every team.

Spread that feedback as compost over your entire team to slow down conflict in the future. As compost slows down the growth of weeds, retains moisture and feeds nutrients into the soil, feedback works similarly by slowing down conflict, allowing for reflection and building motivation in your team.

Those mind mapping sessions are great feedback tools too. They are to be used again and again to quickly dive into challenging areas and clarify issues. Please remember to use mind mapping regularly, it is a wonderful tool.

Recycling - don't waste anything. Every experience and interaction is a learning opportunity which you can capitalise on in the future. You learn from good and bad experiences, acquiring knowledge, expertise and data to put into practice in the future. A good gardener throws very little away, they reuse whatever they can, so remember as you nurture your team to draw on events from the past, and develop them into good practices for the future.

# Continuity and producing a consistent approach

Continuity, perseverance, persistence, dedication and endurance are all required from you to maintain and improve your team. The goal of this book has been to provide you with tools and information to help you improve your team's productivity by reducing workplace conflict. Nothing I've said will make any improvement in your world unless you stick at it and maintain the standards you put on yourself. I cannot do the work or set those standards for you, it is up to you to stick with the game plan you set, and continue when the going gets tough. Don't let others distract you from your plan, have those timelines visible where you and others will see them to remain accountable.

Gardening is a long term project, just like your work on increasing productivity in your team. Don't expect dramatic results overnight, the results will come, but need ongoing work and a consistent approach over the long term.

We spend hundreds of hours at work every year and it's very easy to get side-tracked with shiny object syndrome from time to time. Just remember that your goal is to improve productivity which will in turn improve your life. Stick to your goals and refer back to them when you realise you are heading off-track. You are working on your long term management development which will become your management style to achieve these improvements.

## Reaping the rewards

If you haven't started already, now is the time for you to put the concepts and models to work. There is no time like the present to get to work on improving your team's productivity. Don't leave what you have learnt now for another day, now is your time for action.

The concepts I have been talking about throughout the book do take time and effort. The work to get the results can be difficult, but the results are very rewarding.

Positive bottom line results come from increased productivity, which is incremental; something you work on every day, but only see the results when you step back and take in the bigger picture. It is similar in gardening as you spend hours working on the detail. You plan, weed, plant and fertilise, then later you get to sit back and enjoy what you have created and the fruits of your labour.

You will have also created a more comfortable place to work in. By reducing conflict in your team, the stress-relief that people experience changes the whole workplace atmosphere and staff can enjoy coming into work and spending time with their teammates. People spend a large portion of their life at work, some 1848 hours every year in Australia, so the better the environment you create, the more productive and effective your staff will be.

With more productive and effective staff you can accomplish better results because of your greater respect and trust in each other. Conversations now focus on being the best you can be, rather than solving conflict or gossiping about it. New ideas can be shared and developed together. What better way to spend the extra time you created through reducing conflict than to create new concepts, products and improvements.

While you are enjoying this new improved working environment, share it with others. Colleagues will have already noticed the improvements in your team and may start asking you for advice. Hopefully family and friends are also noticing an improved change in you, as reduced stress levels begin to flow into all areas of your life. Your work is not an isolated, stand-alone compartment; what happens in that environment affects the other aspects of your life. With improvement in your professional life, your personal life will improve too.

## Here to help

Well done again in making it to the end of my book. Thanks for sticking with me and taking the time to read all the way through. I really do hope that you have picked up some valuable tools on the way and that you will put them into practice.

If you would like more information on anything discussed in this book please drop me a line at malguy@mimmediation.net, or visit my website www.mimmediation.net

Apart from my mediation practice, my services also comprise of seminars and presentations, including:

\*         **Conflict Mind-Mapping**

    -    Establishing a roadmap to identify and deal with existing issues

\*         **Policy and Procedure Audits**

    -    A check-up of current company documents and practices

\*         **First Aid for Conflict**

    -    How to respond to conflict in the first instance

* **In-Depth 5 day Conflict Resolution Programs**

    - Tailored to your company for your specific needs

* **Conference Speaking Engagements**

    - Focusing on reducing workplace conflict and increasing productivity.

Drop me a line with any question; I'd love to work with you to increase productivity in your workplace.

I am here to help.

## In Closing

I know several CEO's who enjoy nothing better than spending time in their gardens, away from the office and pressures that revolve around them. They enjoy the quiet time while engaging with nature itself, and propagating their own little corner of their world, just as they want.

Jeff Kennett, former Premier of Victoria and now chairman of Beyond Blue, revealed in March 2015 that he has found enjoyment and stress relief in the working in his garden for many years. He has a relaxed, friendly garden which his family and friends can enjoy for many more years to come. A garden will always require maintenance, but once established, the ongoing requirements can be managed with simplicity.

Kennett said, "When I was Premier and I had a lot on my plate, I did my clearest thinking in the garden. There was no one around me, no demands, no telephone calls, no papers to be signed. It fits in with my philosophical approach to life. I think gardening is very important to relieve stress and anxiety. I've done it all my life. It's been a very important balance."

Your workplace can be an enjoyable environment to work in too, just as many enjoy working in their garden. How you cultivate and develop your culture and environment is up to you, and while not everything in it is within your control, even people living in the harshest of climates often create something of a garden with what they are given.

Under the right circumstances including time, healthy conditions, people and the appropriate knowledge you can generate a remarkably productive environment, and all the wonderful outcomes that go with it.

## One final quote from Albert Einstein,

"I never teach my pupils. I only attempt to provide the conditions in which they can learn."

# Bibliography

1. The Mediation Institute
http://www.mediationinstitute.edu.au/

2. Top 10 reasons why employees quit their jobs.
http://humanresources.about.com/od/resigning-from-your-job/a/top-10-reasons-employees-quit-their-job.htm

3. Forbes article – 'Why are your employees leaving?'

   http://www.forbes.com/sites#/sites/reneesylvestrewilliams/2012/01/30/why-your-employees-are-leaving/

4. Cost of employee turnover calculator - https://au.drakeintl.com/hr-news/cost-of-turnover-calculator.aspx

5. Anti bullying benchbook from Fair Work Commission
http://benchbooks.fwc.gov.au/antibullying/assets/File/ABBenchbook.pdf

6. Simple Plan Lyrics http://www.metrolyrics.com/welcome-to-my-life-lyrics-simple-plan.html

7. Lorene Schaefer's blog http://winwinhr.com/the-continuum-of-dispute-resolution-in-the-workplace/

8. Lorene Schaefer  www.workplacegroupusa.com

9. Dr Tammy Lenski  http://lenski.com

10. Fair Work Ombudsman Australia  https://www.fairwork.gov.au/

11. Mediation Institute  http://mediationinstitute.com.au/

12. Malcolm Guy  www.mimmediation.net

13. Clinton Swaine,  www.frontiertrainings.com

14. Scott Guy: His Parents Story  http://www.amazon.com.au/Scott-Guy-Parents-Betrayal-Courage-ebook/dp/B00GRXV1ZC/ref=cm_cr_pr_pb_opt?ie=UTF8

15. Joanne and Anna Guy's blog site  http://makelemonade.co.nz/

www.ingramcontent.com/pod-product-compliance
Lightning Source LLC
Chambersburg PA
CBHW021429170526
45164CB00001B/161